SEPECAT

JAGUAR

ENDANGERED SPECIES

CONTENTS

FOREWORD

THE IMPENDING RETIREMENT of the Jaguar is of great sadness to many and is particularly poignant in my life as Station Commander at RAF Coltishall, a station that is unequivocally linked to the aircraft. In fact, Coltishall can be considered as home to the Jaguar, the type having operated from the base for over thirty years – almost half of the station's history. Of equal sadness is the closure of the station itself, one of the last former RAF Battle of Britain airfields to have remained active.

That said, the Jaguar has served the RAF well and has successfully embraced change with its ability to adapt in not only role but also in technological advance. It could be said that it is a very different aircraft today than the one I began flying twenty or so years ago.

This book, through its illustrations, goes a long way in recording the history of the Jaguar, from the Cold War in its strike attack role to that of close air support today, from low-level delivery and reconnaissance in the late twentieth century to medium-level accuracy in the twenty-first.

I first met the author in 1988 when he was researching an article on Jaguar tactical reconnaissance. At that time I was nearing the end of my first tour on the aircraft. The photographs he produced on that occasion were stunning and this portfolio is a testament to his ability with the camera.

This book serves as a great memento to the aircraft for both the servicemen who have been so closely connected with it, the enthusiast who will find most, if not all, the variations of schemes that it has operated in, and to the photographer for the stunning images.

Graham Wright OBE BSc MRAeS
Air Commodore, RAF

INTRODUCTION

THE DEMISE OF any front line aircraft will always bring an abundance of sadness from those who have operated it as well as from those on the outside, who have been equally fascinated by its mystique and aura, and the sense that it is that little bit untouchable. We lament the passing of many significant types in RAF service, from the Vickers Supermarine Spitfire to the Hawker Hunter and the English Electric Lightning, all of which have their own charisma and which have been responsible for this country's survival for well over half a century. As nostalgic as this may be, for many of us the stories and histories are distant, belonging to another era. Many historians, enthusiasts and photographers today are captivated by more recent designs, many of which have proven themselves very capable war fighting platforms and have carved their own niche in history.

Sepecat Jaguar is one of those types. An aircraft that was born out a political defence procurement shambles involving the BAC TSR2, its supposed replacement in the shape of the General Dynamics F-111K, the UK re-design of the perfectly configured McDonnell F-4 Phantom II, and the last gasp stop-gap measure of re-rolling the Blackburn/HAS Buccaneer to meet the perceived overland threat.

In Jaguar, the Air Staff and those tasked with identifying the future operational requirement within the Ministry of Defence gained a small low-level interdictor capable of operating in all weathers and at night, a capability hitherto absent from the then front line RAF inventory.

Ironically, the Jaguar design began life as a two-seat supersonic trainer conceived as a possible replacement for the Folland Gnat. Jeffery Quill, then with the British Aerospace Corporation (BAC), who will no doubt be remembered for his testing days with Vickers Supermarine rather than as sales director for SEPECAT, the joint Anglo-French company responsible for the Jaguar concept, recalled in an interview that:

In Britain the need for a replacement for the Gnat was brewing up. The idea of international collaborations in aerospace was also very popular. There was a lot of thought about the Gnat

replacement going on up at B.A.C. Warton, and the idea emerged that the new trainer would be a supersonic aeroplane, Mach 1.2-1.3. Over in France there was another requirement called the ECAT for a small operational trainer with an additional role as a light attack aircraft. Breguet ultimately won the ECAT competition in France.

In Britain, however, you couldn't get a place like Warton drawing lines on bits of paper for a Mach 1.3 two-seat trainer without them closely examining operational roles for it and thinking of hanging weapons on it.

With similar thought on both sides of the channel, international collaboration high on the agenda, and the political will to support such a joint project through the then Minister of Defence Peter Thorneycroft and Messmer, his opposite number in France, the Jaguar was born. Although perhaps uncomfortable with the idea, the two Air Staffs were told to talk to one another to produce a jointly agreed requirement and, whilst there would always be a divide in ultimate ability, the RAF got a platform that would meet their operational requirement of the time and have room for significant growth.

This book is a testament to the Jaguar and in particular its use in RAF service. I do not intend to re-write the many good books

The second French prototype, E02, undertook much of the development flying both in France and in the UK. Its latter years, from 1971 until its last flight on 28 February 1979, were spent on Warton-assigned development taskings.

The first British prototype, XW560, undertook its first flight on 12 October 1969, but its development career was short-lived when, prior to its 367th flight on 11 August 1972 from Boscombe Down back to Warton, at the hands of Paul Millett, it suffered a rear-end fire on the runway.

at low-level in Cumbria between Grasmere and Thirlemere Lakes, I get a large twinge of envy at the crew encased in their high-demand working environment.

Unlike many other photographers and enthusiasts, I have been fortunate enough to be allowed significant access to the aircraft in its operational environment due to having worked in defence journalism for twenty years. From this access and both my passion for aviation and for the aircraft itself I have amassed a considerable Jaguar portfolio. This I now hope to share, intermixed with some personal experiences and some historical facts, to provide the reader with an everlasting memento of one of the RAF's most formidable front line platforms of the Cold War era.

PHOTOGRAPHIC PLATFORM

and articles so far produced on the aircraft or to delve into the mysteries of design, development and growth. It has come simply from my association with the jet over its entire life cycle, something I could not possibly contemplate with any other platform in spite of my fascination for the likes of Spitfire, Hunter or Lightning. I must, however, offer thanks to the many service personnel and close friends who have been instrumental in helping me over the years, in particular Eric Bucklow, Martin Kaye, Jim Britton and Graham Green at the BAE SYSTEMS Historical Branch, who provided a number of photographs and some of the information.

Jaguar first appeared on the public scene in June 1969 when the second French prototype, E02, was displayed at the Paris Salon. In Britain, it was at the SBAC show at Farnborough the following year that Jaguar made its debut. The French prototype was present, along with XW560, the first British prototype, which had undertaken its maiden flight on 12 October 1969.

My association with the Jaguar began two years later, again at Farnborough. On this occasion, three examples were evident: XW563 and XW566, the two UK prototypes, as well as the French E02. At that time I was captivated; thirty-four years later every time I gaze at the small shape as it winds through the Welsh valleys of the Machynlleth Loop or slices through Dunmail Raise

With somewhere in the region of 140 hours of front line fast-jet flying behind me, not to mention several hundred hours working from less nimble platforms, I feel that I am quite well qualified to assess the merits of air-to-air photography and in particular the confines of an environment not specifically designed for my needs.

Once back in 1996, when I was visiting Kuantan Air Base, Royal Malaysian Air Force, during a five nation IADS exercise, I was talking to a group of Royal New Zealand Air Force pilots from No.75 Squadron. The merits of the discussion were photo opportunities the following day when their six ship of Douglas A-4K Skyhawk aircraft would be taking on fuel from the RAF VC-10 tanker aircraft that I would be flying on over the South China Sea. Having 'briefed' a number of formation changes I was asked what was the best aircraft I had ever flown in. Without hesitation or thinking how the question was directed, I remarked Jaguar. Not that it was the most formidable or demanding platform I had ever had the privilege to fly in but because it was such a good photographic platform.

In clarification and in my defence I stated I had not flown the 'Scooter', as the Skyhawk was affectionately known, but that I favoured Jaguar because it had a two-piece canopy that was less prone to reflections inside the cockpit. It had a very small wing set behind the cockpit and small intakes so as not to obscure sideways, back or downward visibility and it had sufficient punch to encompass most operating attitudes within the flight envelope and had power to spare. My straightforward answer must have impressed because the following day's photo-shoot went without a hitch and it was only later that I was to find that the lead pilot, from whom the question originated, was an RAF Jaguar pilot on an exchange posting. Certainly a case of saying the right thing at the right time!

Although those attributes so evident to me as a photographer were perhaps not those which drove the design of the Jaguar, they were clearly a plus to the crews that were to operate the system and perhaps went some way in making the Jaguar such a successful design. Certainly those pilots I have had the privilege to fly with and those that I have known socially have nothing but praise for the jet. Equally, although it is now an old design involving 1960s technology, Jaguar has had the ability to absorb many upgrades to keep it at the cutting edge of front line technology. As many people involved with the aircraft will be quick to point out, the aircraft has pioneered many advances that have been absorbed into newer and already more advanced platforms.

I spare no regret in predominantly directing this book towards the Royal Air Force use of the jet. It is not because the Anglo–French collaboration turned out to be somewhat one-sided following Dassault's take-over of Breguet, or that the French opted not to develop the Jaguar as much as the RAF. It is simply that it was made in Britain for Britain and everything else becomes an also-ran.

The Armee d'L'Air has already retired its Jaguars and the Nigerian Air Force has not flown its examples for a number of years and now probably never will. Here in the United Kingdom we have another year before the aircraft passes into history, although our exports elsewhere to such places as Ecuador, Oman and India will keep the jet flying for the best part of the next decade. I hope, therefore, that through my photographs this book will provide a lasting memento for all those who have an affection for the jet.

Peter R. Foster
Doddington, Cambs 2006

Above From a personal viewpoint, the Jaguar was probably the ideal cockpit in which to work. Lacking large intakes, and with a small wing, the aircraft provided the ideal photographic platform.

Left Low level is the Jaguar's bread and butter environment. It has only been in its twilight years, with the introduction of smart weapons, that the aircraft has found itself operating more at medium level. Here a No.41 (F) Squadron Jaguar GR.1A skips through the Cumbrian hills.

The first twenty-two production Jaguar GR.1s were delivered with the characteristic 'French' nose, lacking the 'chisel' shape of later aircraft incorporating the 'LRMTS'. This batch was delivered to both 226 OCU and No.54 Squadron, although the aircraft were retro-fitted later.

CHAPTER 1
HUMBLE BEGINNINGS AND UPGRADE

IT HAS BEEN said recently that today, some thirty years since its first flight, the front third of the Jaguar is at the cutting edge of technology but the age of the remainder is its Achilles heel. Probably not a truer word has been said and I recall quite vividly talking to Lt-Col. Jacek Lazarczyk, the commander of 7 ELT, Polish Air Force, who said during a recent visit his unit made to RAF Coltishall that he found the Jaguar technically superior to his own Sukhoi Su22 M4 'Fitter Ks', but the bigger Soviet design was in his opinion a much better platform, given that the same upgrades in avionics would be a force to be reckoned with.

When Jaguar started out in the early 1970s it was perhaps the most glamorous aircraft in the RAF's inventory. Sir Jock Stirrup, former Chief of the Air Staff and current Chief of the Defence Staff, recounted at a 2005 IDMA dinner a visit he made to Farnborough when still at Cranwell on pilot training. That day he watched the BAC test pilot put the jet through its paces and marvelled at its agility. At that point he made a wish that one day he would get to fly the aircraft. Two tours as an instructor with 226 OCU and two front line tours with Nos II (AC) and 41 (F) Squadrons later, he still holds the jet in his highest esteem. Although, as a realist, his has become the final decision on the type's future.

As a photographer I perhaps view the Jaguar somewhat differently from the highly skilled pilots and technicians who operate it. Standing on the side of mountains in the UK's main low-flying areas and watching the small sleek shape of the Jaguar as it twists and turns through the various passes and rolling inverted over the crests you could be forgiven for thinking that it possesses the most sophisticated of terrain-following systems. Yet in fact the Jaguar has no radar at all, relying solely on pilot skill and the inertial navigation and attack system. It is even more incredible that the pilots are expected to accomplish this in practically all weathers and at night too!

The initial RAF production Jaguar was powered by two Adour Mk 102 turbofans, each developing 5,115lb st (22.8 kN) dry and

7,304lb st (32.5kN) with reheat. The differences between the single-seat GR.1 and twin-seat T.2 were, apart from the obvious, limited to the lack of a LRMTS (Laser Ranger and Marked Target Seeker) nose, an in-flight refuelling capability, and RWR. The remainder was built to a common standard.

The avionics comprised HUD, radar altimeter, E2B compass and auto-stabilisation system from Smiths; Plessy V/UHF and HF/UHF radios and stores management system; Cosser ILS: IFF; TACAN; Elliot air data computer; Ferranti and Marconi–Elliot nav/attack system.

At the birth of Jaguar the Marconi-Elliot NAVWASS (Navigation & Weapon Aiming System), including an E3R inertial platform and MSC 920M computer-linked to the HUD with a 'head-down' map display, was considered remarkable. However, the true beauty of Jaguar was its ability to absorb upgrades. The first of these came in 1978 with the introduction of the Mk 104 version of the Adour turbofan that already equipped export aircraft. Beginning with

The ETPS used the twin-seat Jaguar successfully for nearly thirty years as a high-speed, high-demand training platform for its students. Attrition for such a small unit was high, with two out of five dedicated platforms being lost in accidents. Here, the unit's final Jaguar T.2A, ZB615, is seen negotiating the Machynlleth loop.

Jaguars assigned to RAF Germany, the Mk 104 offered increased thrust of 5,270lb st (23kN) dry and 7,900lb st (36kN) in reheat, although, during operations in the Gulf War, turbine temperatures were allowed to rise from 700 to 725°C, boosting figures to 5,300lb st (24kN) and 8,100lb st (36kN). At the front end the NAVWASS was replaced by the even better Ferranti FIN 1064, comprising a new INS, computer and power supply, linked to the

existing radar altimeter, air data computer, HUD, moving map display and laser ranger. On top of this, the new system offered a weight saving of 110lb (50kg) and occupied only one third of the space. This brought about the first designation change, to Jaguar GR.1A and T.2A respectively, with an initial seventy-five single-seat and sixteen two-seat aircraft receiving the modification.

Various external self-defence aids were also added during the 1980s, many already having been adopted on export models. These included the Philips-MATRA Phimat chaff pod, Tracer AN/ALE-40 flare dispensers, Westinghouse AN/ALQ-101 (V) jamming pods and provision for the conveyance of AIM-9L Sidewinder air-to-air missiles. The provision of over-wing missile rails were added in response to the need posed by the first Gulf War.

With the introduction of Tornado GR.1 as a replacement for the Jaguar aircraft assigned to Royal Air Force Germany in the low-level interdiction strike/attack role, followed by the end of the Cold War, the Jaguar was seen in some quarters as an aircraft that had 'had its time' and now had a limited life expectancy. But even the darkest of events often have a silver lining. The Iraqi invasion of Kuwait and the resulting Operation Granby demonstrated the Jaguar's ability to be rapidly deployed 'out of area' – its reliability, ruggedness and maintainability whilst operating away from a main base infrastructure.

'Granby' modifications undertaken at the JMU between August and October 1990 saw a number of aircraft (twelve were deployed) receive over-wing missile rails for AIM-9L sidewinders, some radar 'stealth' (RCS reduction) measures including Surface Wave Absorbent Material (SWAM) on the leading edges and Radar Absorbent Material (RAM) tiles in the intakes. The Jaguars were equipped with new or revised IFF communications and EW equipment, and received rapid clearance to operate a range of new weapons. The initial trials were undertaken at Boscombe Down, utilising aircraft XZ385.

Later, to enable the RAF to undertake operations over the former Yugoslavia, a requirement was drawn up for the additional use of autonomous laser designators, Tornado having already service-tested TIALD (Thermal Imaging Airborne Laser Designator) under operational conditions. An Urgent Operation Requirement (UOR) was therefore issued to provide this capability and, for a number of reasons, Jaguar was selected as the most appropriate platform at the time.

Jaguar T.2A XX833 belonging to DERA (Defence Evaluation & Research Agency) at Boscombe Down and operated on behalf of the CTTO (Central Tactics & Trials Organisation) had already been integrated with TIALD as part of the ongoing research programme investigating the feasibility of using the laser designator in a single-seat platform.

A trial installation in a single Jaguar GR.1A was undertaken as Boscombe Down and this integration was put into production for a planned ten single-seat Jaguar GR.1As and two T.2As. A second proof installation aircraft was then converted by a team from St Athan under the guidance of Boscombe Down. St Athan then produced six more single-seaters and the two twin-seaters. The last (tenth) modification was not completed, and the aircraft instead became the prototype Jaguar 96.

Operated under a deviation to the Jaguar GR.1A release to service, there should have been no designation change. The aircraft were, however, widely known as Jaguar GR.1B, and, later, as more aircraft received upgrades, the GR.1A(T). The eleven modified aircraft incorporated a MIL STD 1553B digital databus and received a new Smiths multi-purpose colour HDD that could be used to display either a digital moving map or TIALD imagery. Other upgrades to improve navigational accuracy were also added, and the opportunity to 'tidy up' the Jaguar cockpit was also taken. The first flight in this configuration was undertaken on 11 January 1995 with the first missions over Bosnia taking place five months later on 27 May 1995.

Such was the success of the upgrade, and with a probable delay to Typhoon's service entry, the decision was made to upgrade the bulk of the single-seat Jaguar force to the same standard through a staged upgrade. The twin-seat T.2A would receive some improvements but, lacking LRMTS, in-flight refuelling and RWR, would not be in a position to be used operationally.

The first stage saw the evolution of Jaguar 96, which included the full package of modifications applied to the aircraft used in Operation Granby, the installation of a MIL STD 1553B databus, wide-angle HUD, improved RWR and navigation suite, complementing the GPS-embedded FIN 1064C INAS. This allowed all Jaguar 96 aircraft to carry TIALD and to be fitted with the GR.1B-type display screen. Akin to GR.1B, Jaguar 96 was operated in service by a deviation to the Jaguar GR.1A's release to service and, as such, saw no type re-designation. Ultimately, when

a new and separate Military Aircraft Release was issued, the jets were re-designated Jaguar GR.3 and T.4 respectively.

The second staged upgrade, Jaguar 97, saw the aircraft receive a new state of the art multi-function LCD display to present TIALD imagery and a moving map display. It was a display larger than that introduced in Jaguar 96, with better fidelity. On top of this, there was the introduction of a helmet-mounted sighting system, integrating both the sighting of the TIALD sensor and the aircraft's Sidewinder AAM, allowing the pilot to engage off-boresight air-to-air targets. Wiring for operation of ASRAAM was also provided as part of the upgrade.

AAMs were very much a secondary addition to the Jaguar's main purpose in life, and the software improvements leaned very much towards more accurate aiming of the Paveway II and Paveway III LGBs, as well as allowing TIALD to be used to measure slant range instead of the laser rangefinder. Finally, the jet would also be able to carry the then new 'Jaguar Replacement Reconnaissance Pod' (JRRP), later referred to as the 'Joint Reconnaissance Pod' (JRP), a development of Vinten's existing Series 18 Type 601 GP(1) pod,

Much of the Jaguar development and upgrade was conducted jointly between the manufacturer and the Ministry of Defence. The creation of the Strike Attack Operational Evaluation Unit (SAOEU) did much to enhance the programme, providing a more defined two-way link between front-end user and the manufacturer. Here, two jets, XX723 and XX725, are seen in formation while en route from Boscombe Down to the US Naval Weapons Centre at China Lake as part of the unit's annual 'Highrider' trials programme.

utilising electro-optical sensors instead of wet film cameras. From this, Jaguar 97 was to become Jaguar GR.3A, the final type change. Aircraft XZ399 was flown to BAE SYSTEMS at Warton and, on 27 January 1999, undertook its maiden flight in this configuration. This was followed by XX116, the second proof installation aircraft from Boscombe Down upgraded by a team from St Athan.

This is not the end of Jaguar upgrades. Another big item on the Jaguar pilot's wish list has always been more power. To this end the turn of the century saw a programme introduced to replace the aircraft's existing Adour Mk 104 with the Mk 106. The Adour Mk 106 would take the cold section from the T–45 Goshawks Adour Mk 871 and the reheat section of the Jaguars Mk 811, giving the jet approximately 25 per cent greater thrust. By using parts of the existing engine with the new cold section it was seen as a programme designed as a spend-to-save measure. The Mk 104 was becoming increasingly difficult and expensive to support and thus a reduction in maintenance costs would effectively save money in the longer term.

The first production Jaguar GR.1, XX108, still assigned to the company trials fleet, was the first jet to receive the Mk 106 upgrade and carried out much of the engine integration work. Fittingly, XZ400, the final RAF production single-seat was flown to Warton, following upgrade to GR.3 at St Athan in May 2000, to join XX108 as part of the trials fleet. It was re-delivered back to RAF Coltishall on 24 January 2002 as the first production engine upgrade.

While improvements in the front third of the Jaguar could continue almost unabated, the back section, through both fatigue and 1960s design had perhaps been taken as far as economically it could. That said, Jaguar still provides the RAF with a front line deployable entity that is the envy of the world.

CHAPTER 2

PRODUCTION TESTING
A Bad Day at the Office

An interview with Senior BAE SYSTEMS Production Test Pilot
Eric Bucklow on his first flight in Omani AF aircraft 201

By the first flight of OB1, the first Omani trainer, on 4 November 1976 I had undertaken seventy Jaguar first flights so things had become fairly routine. It was one of the usual 'wait all day' for the aeroplane days, which eventually became ready quite late in the afternoon, just in time to get the first flight. Myself and Vic Malings went off and one of the first things we used to do on a production flight was to invert the aircraft to shake out any pencils, swarf and other rubbish that the people building the plane might have left in it. We did this at about 5,000 feet, got the right way up, and I then found that the stick wouldn't come back any further than about neutral. It was OK as long as we kept the speed up but if we tried to slow down then we could not keep the nose up. At this stage Air Traffic asked for a report of weather conditions, so I gave a good run down on the cloud layers which amused people afterwards as they thought this was a cool thing to do with the controls jammed, but they weren't really jammed.

We then started to consider what we could do in terms of landing the aircraft and obviously it was going to be a fairly high speed landing because if you lowered the flaps, even if we could have got down to the flap limiting speed. The flaps actually introduce the nose down trim change anyway, so we needed to further back stick with the flaps down than we would with the flaps up. We were therefore looking at a 250 knot landing with no flaps, which did not sound very healthy.

We sat and thought about it for a while and at that stage the left re-heat warning came on. The fire warning system on the Jaguar at that stage was giving a lot of spurious warnings. However, we shut the engine down and took the correct action on that. I think

Before delivery, each aircraft has to pass through a rigorous acceptance procedure at the hands of the company test pilots. Here, Eric Bucklow is presented with a memento to mark his 100th first flight in a Jaguar. The jet concerned was 'OS10', pictured here in the background, and this was to later feature prominently in the history of the Jaguar.

SEPECAT JAGUAR ENDANGERED SPECIES

Year 1976		AIRCRAFT		Captain or 1st Pilot	Co-pilot 2nd Pilot Pupil or Crew	DUTY (including number of day or night landings as 1st Pilot or Dual)	Day Flying 1st Pilot (1)	2nd Pilot (2)
Month	Date	Type and Mark	No.					
—	—	—	—	—	—	Totals brought forward	4304-35	
NOV	4	JAG INT	BO1	SELF	MALINGS	P.1	40	
	8	CANB T.17	WH863		BEVAN MALINGS	P.1	55	
	10	JAG GR.1	X2372			P.1	1-05	
	11	"	"			P.2	1-00	
	12	"	"			P.3	30	
	12	CANB T.17	WH863		WOOLLETT	P.2	50	
	15	"	"		MAUNES	P.3	40	
	16	"	"		KENWARD	P.4	30	
	26	BAC 167/80A	G-27-296		AITKEN	P.2	50	
	29	CANB T.4	WJ869		EVANS	P.4	25	
	29	BAC 167/80A	G-27-296		KENWARD	P.3	45	
	30	JAG GR.1	X2371			P.8	20	
DEC	1	CESS 402B	G-BADT		EVANS	WTN-HAWARDEN-NORTHOLT-WTN	1-35	
	7	JAG INT	SE1			P.8	35	
	9	JAG GR.1	X2374			P.1	1-10	
	14	JAG INT	SE2			P.1	15	
	16	"	"			P.2	1-35	
	16	JAG GR.1	X2375			P.1	1-05	
	23	"	"			P.2	50	
	31	CHEROKEE	G-BASL		S+P BUCKLOW	LOCAL FLYING	25	
	31	"	"		S+A "	"	15	
						Totals carried forward	4320-50	
							(1)	(2)

An extract from Eric Bucklow's flying logbook, with the almost matter of fact entry on his first flight in 'OB1', described elsewhere.

on my first Jaguar solo, I got one, which was quite a surprise, it certainly had been occurring throughout those years from 1973-ish. I am not quite sure when it was fixed. The fire wire itself was the cause of the problem. When subject to dampness and things like that it would set off the warning. I presume that in later years it was fixed because you could not have lived with it forever. Generally speaking, however, after four or five flights the system appeared to settle itself down but I assume a permanent fix was found in the end.

We then thought of ways of getting round the control restriction. Probably the fist thing to try was turn the aircraft upside down again, in case something was jammed in the control runs to see if we could shake it free. This we did and after a bit of vigorous pumping around with the stick, upside down, turned it back right side up and lo and behold, the restriction had cleared. That was that problem solved. We decided at that point to recover to Warton on the one engine and of course, by that time operations had decided there was some sort of emergency. They alerted the fire crews and the result of that due to their keenness was that the airfield was covered with fire engines, leaving the runway as the narrow track to get between everything. On final approach, we selected to lower flaps but the flaps refused to come down, so at this stage I was beginning to wonder what was happening at the back end. However, we eventually recovered to Warton in a one-engine high-ish speed landing and managed to avoid all the fire engines.

The subsequent investigation afterwards established that the three failures were all totally unrelated and that the control jam was due to a largish rivet getting stuck in the area where the mixing of lateral and pitch commands occurs for the differential tail. The events as they unfolded that afternoon left us examining a number of possibilities and at one stage we had considered diverting to Boscombe Down to take advantage of its longer runway and I think we would have had a go at putting it down at the 250 knot mark and seeing what happened at the end of the runway.

If we had not been able to have freed the controls we would have had to have made the approach at a speed which you still had a little bit of back stick available, so we could have flared the aeroplane in that final stage. Of course, that would have meant a fairly high-speed arrival. A landing without flaps, should we either not have been able to lower them or because of the speed limiting factor, was not the major issue as a flapless landing does give you more pitch control. Obviously, the initial problem affecting pitch control was the overriding concern.

CHAPTER 3
RAF STATIONS AND SQUADRONS

RAF LOSSIEMOUTH

Jaguar arrived at RAF Lossiemouth on 30 May 1973 when the fourth production GR.1, XX111, was flown in from Warton. This was followed closely by three further single-seat examples before the arrival of the first twin-seater. This was XX137, the second production aircraft. At its height, the unit, at that time simply referred to as the Jaguar OCU, had nearly fifty aircraft on strength.

The station itself was built during 1938 and 1939 and opened on 1 May 1939 with No.15 Flying Training School as the major unit. In April 1940, the station was handed over to Bomber Command and No.20 Operational Training Unit was formed together with No.46 Maintenance Unit.

At the end of the Second World War, Lossiemouth became a satellite of RAF Milltown in Coastal Command, before becoming HMS Fulmar of the Royal Navy in 1946, the primary task being Fleet Air Arm operations.

With the impending demise of aircraft carriers and the drawdown in Royal Navy fixed wing operations, the RAF returned on 28 September 1972 and the station steadily assumed greater status since then. Aircraft types that have operated from here over the following three decades have included Gannet AEW.3, the final Royal Navy unit, Whirlwind HAR.10, Jaguar GR.1/3/ T.2/4, Shackleton AEW.2, Sea King HAR.3, Hunter T.7A/8C, Buccaneer S.2B and Tornado GR.1/4, employed in various roles including search and rescue, airborne early warning, operational conversion, tactical weapons training and maritime strike/attack. Ground-based units have included the air and ground defence, airfield damage repair and airfield support roles.

The Jaguar was to leave Lossiemouth on 21 July 2000 when the type was consolidated at RAF Coltishall. Today, with its present Tornado GR.4 complement of three operational units (Nos 12,

14 and 617 Squadrons), one operational conversion unit (No.XV (Reserve) Squadron) and its Westland Sea King HAR.3 helicopter search and rescue unit ('D' Flight), No.202 Squadron, and two ground defence units (Nos 51 and 2622 (Highland Squadrons), RAF Regiment, RAF Lossiemouth is one of the foremost stations in the Royal Air Force.

Initial Jaguar deliveries were to RAF Lossiemouth, where No.226 OCU was re-formed to oversee all Jaguar training. Two separate squadrons formed within the OCU and, at its height, it boasted nearly fifty aeroplanes. The shot seen here, from the ATC control tower at RAF Lossiemouth, depicts No.2 Squadron/226 OCU.

Above Jaguar GR.1 XX117 '05' of 226 OCU seen at RAF Lossiemouth in August 1975. The aircraft at this time retained the 'French' nose and lacked the in-flight refuelling probe introduced on the fourteenth production aircraft. Its time with the OCU was limited as it was selected to become one of the aircraft to be loaned to India.

Below Wrap-around camouflage on the Jaguar began being applied in early 1976 at RAF Kemble. The crossed quiver and flaming torch markings were introduced in 1977 and were first applied to XX759. The Lumsden tartan fin bands appeared in 1981. XX752 '06' 226 OCU is seen here at RAF Mildenhall in May 1982 in pristine condition.

226 Operational Conversion Unit

226 OCU was initially formed at Molesworth, within the structure of No.11 Group on 15 August 1946 to train fighter pilots from the re-structuring of No.1335 Conversion Unit, then equipped with a variety of types including Tempests, Hornets, Meteors and Vampires. The unit disbanded at Driffield, being renamed No.203 Advanced Flying School on 31 August 1949, by which time it had been re-assigned to No.21 Group.

It was resurrected again in No.12 Group by the renaming No.203 AFS at Stradishall to train Meteor pilots, only to transfer to No.11 Group again for a short period, before another period of inactivity on 3 June 1955.

Its number plate stood up again by renaming the Lightning Conversion Squadron at Middleton St George on 1 June 1963, before its re-location to RAF Coltishall. It disbanded at Coltishall on 30 September 1974 and stood up the following day by renaming the Jaguar Conversion Unit at Lossiemouth on 1 October 1974. However, in an effort to preserve the dwindling RAF squadron number plates, it was disbanded again by being renamed No.16 (Reserve) Squadron on 1 November 1991.

Above In the 1970s, with the Jaguar at the cutting edge of technology, the RAF was keen to show it off. In recent times, second line units have supplied crews for display routines and therefore this task was undertaken by 226OCU. Here, aircraft XX763 is seen taxiing at the start of its display routine at RAF Valley in August 1979. The jet has received the quiver and flaming torch motif but lacks the tartan stripe across the RWR.

Jaguar GR.1A XX116 '02' 226 OCU seen low-level in Scotland. The aircraft was to spend much of its career on strength of the training unit although it participated in the Indian Air Force loan programme. It was later to become the second Jaguar 97 trials aircraft.

At its height at RAF Lossiemouth, 226 OCU was to operate almost fifty aircraft split into Squadrons 1 and 2. The unit was to roll-out eight front line units for the Royal Air Force over the next five years, not to mention an extensive training program for overseas customers of the Jaguar, before settling in to the steady trade of re-supply to the front line. No.1 Squadron 226 OCU disbanded on 31 March 1979. Initially with such a high turnover of aircraft, many squadrons training on their own jets under the auspice of the 226 OCU mantle, markings were kept to a minimum.

However, once a more settled complement of aircraft had arrived, an accepted unit insignia was developed. The crossed quiver and flaming torch was derived in 1977, and aircraft XX759 received the first insignia on its vertical stabiliser. Next came the addition of Lumsden tartan fin bands. This arrived in May 1981 and was to remain the trend, along with the accepted individual two number or single letter code, until the unit was re-designated 16 (Reserve) Squadron ten years later.

Motto: 'We Sustain'.

No.16 Squadron

Following an illustrious history, No.16 Squadron came into the Jaguar world following the end of the first Gulf War, the draw down of front line forces after the Cold War, and the warming of East–West relations. In an effort to retain front line RAF number plates, it was decided to re-introduce the practice of aligning operational conversion units and second line training squadrons to a shadow status reflecting the fact that the instructors would form the nucleus of such squadrons in the event of hostilities. It was as a result of this that 226 OCU took on the No.16 (Reserve) Squadron status on 1 November 1991. In Lightning days, it had carried the markings of No.65 Squadron.

No.16 was formed at St Omer in France on 10 February 1915 from detached flights taken from Squadron Nos 2, 5 and 6. As with many squadrons at this time it operated a variety of types until fully equipped with BE2s a year later. No.16 was a Royal Flying Corps reconnaissance unit, carrying out the standard range of operations. RE8s replaced the BE2s in May 1917, which it retained until returning to Britain as a cadre in February 1919, disbanding at Fowlmere on 31 December 1919. During the First World War it was commanded by a number of officers who would achieve Air rank in the future, including Hugh Dowding and 'Peter' Portal.

Limited habitation and relatively good weather are two prime reasons why much of the RAF's low-level tactical training is carried out in Scotland. Therefore 226 OCU and its successor No.16 (Reserve) Squadron remained located at RAF Lossiemouth until it became prudent, economically, to re-locate all the Jaguar aircraft under one roof, so to speak. Here, Jaguar T.2 XX832 is seen crossing Morayshire in October 1995.

Sporting a black fin and the RAF Lossiemouth station crest on the intake, Jaguar GR.1A XX965 lands at RAF Alconbury following a display routing at the then annual 'open house' air show. The aircraft was originally delivered to No.14 Squadron in Germany then, following upgrade, was re-assigned to No.54 Squadron. It was transferred to the OCU on 6 March 1986, with whom it served until retired from service and relegated to ground instructional duties.

As with most RAF squadrons, No.16 was disbanded and re-activated on a number of occasions over the following seventy-odd years as new and old types came and went within the inventory. Equally it was no stranger to either providing the nucleus of new squadrons at its own expense, or itself evolving from other units, as occurred at RAF Lossiemouth with 226 OCU. This is no better described than by events immediately after the Second World War when, from June 1945, the squadron operated a high-speed mail service between Britain and Germany, before having its three flights re-allocated to Squadron Nos 2, 26 and 268 in September, and having the ground staff returned to Dunsford in the UK.

At this point, some confusion exists. On 19 September 1945, both No.487 Squadron and No.268 Squadron were informed that they were now No.16. As a result, 487 was re-numbered 268, and the re-numbering of 268 at Celle remained in place. The squadron continued to operate Spitfire XIXs, XIVs and XVIs until 1 April 1946 when the unit at Celle was disbanded. However, on the same day, No.56 Squadron equipped with Tempest Vs at Fassburg and was re-numbered No.16.

The jet age saw the squadron remain in Germany as part of NATO's front line. For the bulk of that period, it was stationed at RAF Laarbruch, being equipped initially with the Canberra B(I) Mk 8, which it continued to operate until June 1972 when the squadron once again disbanded. On 1 October 1973, No.16

(Designate) Squadron began training in the strike role, equipped with Blackburn Buccaneer S Mk 2s, officially taking over the number plate on 8 January 1973. Buccaneers were operated for the next eleven years continuously from Laarbruch until disbanding on 29 February 1984. However, a new No.16 (Designate) Squadron had begun training at Laarbruch on 1 January 1984, and the day after the Buccaneer unit disbanded, a new Tornado-equipped No.16 Squadron entered service. No.16 remained at Laarbruch with the Tornado GR.1 until the drawdown of RAF Germany. It then became one of the earliest casualties, being disbanded on 11 September 1991. It was just over two months later that it took over the role of front line training of Jaguar pilots at RAF Lossiemouth.

Its tenure at Lossiemouth was to last for just under nine years. In a much scaled down operation from when 226 OCU was operating at capacity, the squadron was now effectively only supporting the provision of new and refreshed aircrew to three front line RAF squadrons, rather than the eight at the height of Jaguar operations. On taking over from 226 OCU, the squadron quite naturally re-introduced their 'Saint' emblem on the tail and 'crossed keys' on the aircraft intakes. In February 1994 it replaced the Lumsden tartan across the aircraft fin with a new Lossiemouth tartan, the first aircraft to sport the change being XX119 '01'. Later the tartan band was to be replaced with one of black outlined in yellow. It was originally intended to re-locate to RAF Coltishall on 1 June 1999 but, as events turned out, the move did not take place until 21 July 2000.

Its operation from RAF Coltishall was to last until March 2005, rather than the originally planned October. Along with No.54 (F) Squadron it was to disband as part of the final farewell to the venerable Jaguar. It was a fitting location in which to complete its Jaguar operations as, though the aircraft has operated elsewhere, Coltishall will always be considered its home. The squadron's task was, however, to remain with the final few aircrew still needing to complete their training. This role was taken on by No.41 Squadron.

Motto: *Operta Aperta* ('Hidden things are revealed')

TRAINING WITH THE JAGUAR

IN AUGUST 1990, when the Royal Air Force dispatched twelve Jaguar GR.1A aircraft and their crews to the Gulf, in response to Iraq's unprovoked attack on Kuwait, they were to be the spearhead of the RAF's involvement in what became Operation Desert Storm. Although this was ultimately a triumph in the application of air power, little were the pilots, or the public, to realise that the Jaguar was to bear the brunt of peacekeeping duties in a number of 'hot spots' almost continuously for the next five years.

Such tales of daring deeds where crews 'go to war', then home for tea and medals, perhaps obscures the fact that none of this would have been possible had it not been for the dedication and professionalism of the Jaguar Operational Conversion Unit (JOCU), later 226 Operational Conversion Unit, and finally No.16 (Reserve) Squadron, as the unit became known. The unit was originally located at RAF Lossiemouth in the far north of Scotland, a base it first moved to some twenty-seven years previously, when the Jaguar was just entering the RAF's inventory.

At that time the unit took on the mantle of No.226 Operational Conversion Unit, a title it received from the previous Lightning Conversion Unit at RAF Coltishall – an appropriate association as this was to be the Jaguar's first operational front line base. With the need to work-up some eight front line squadrons on the type in a four-year period, as well as produce the right training package to meet all the requirements of this new strike/attack aircraft, pilots involved in the program in those early years were to set the very high standard that was maintained throughout its existence.

At that time, when the main threat was still seen as coming from the Warsaw Pact, the Jaguar had a predominantly strike/attack role. Much of this was passed on to the much more sophisticated two-man

When 226 OCU became No.16 (Reserve) Squadron in 1992 it retained the display tasking. As such, aircraft XX116 received this overall black colour scheme with the unit's 'saint' emblem on the fin. This was not the first time the squadron had painted an aircraft in this scheme. When based at RAF Laarbruch operating Buccaneer S.2Bs, an aircraft received a similar scheme, although this lasted just a matter of days.

Tornado GR.4, leaving the Jaguar to concentrate on roles that are more in keeping with the present-day threat scenario of attack and armed reconnaissance.

An aircraft that has been, on more than one occasion, seen as an easy option for politicians attempting to make 'defence savings', survived due to its ability to be such an influential tool of the political will. When many thought it would succumb to inevitable cuts the aircraft and crews have answered by proving just how useful they can be and, as a result, the Jaguar has been continuously upgraded to meet changing roles, increased threats and the introduction of new technology. This has kept the Jaguar in a position where it would be very difficult to be without it, at least until it can be replaced by something better.

Since the early 1970s, No.226 OCU was equipped with as many as twenty-three twin-seat Jaguar T.2s

and twenty-seven single-seat Jaguar GR.1s. No.16 (Reserve) Squadron, which evolved from No.226 OCU, undertook the same task, albeit with a much reduced twelve aircraft. In the first twenty-three years there had been 110 long courses, providing initial conversion for those new to the Jaguar to a level where they were considered at a limited combat-ready state, 121 short courses for those re-entering the Jaguar world or for those moving to positions not requiring the same level of training, and twenty-eight Qualified Weapon Instructor (QWI) courses. On top of this the unit ran its own instructor pilot courses, where experienced pilots were taught how to pass on their knowledge of handling, instrument flying, low-level navigation, weapon delivery, attack profiles and evasion training as detailed in the course syllabus, lasting some seventy hours. A number of other specially tailored

Seen just before the squadron's latest disbandment in March 2005, XX117 sports a very attractive '90th Anniversary' coloured fin. The jet only operated in this guise for a couple of months before the unit deactivated. The jet itself retains the scheme but in a ground instructional role at RAF Cosford.

Small and sleek, the Jaguar is a difficult target for opposing forces. It also has the ability to place ordnance on target with alarming accuracy. Jaguar T.2 XX832 is seen here turning over the North Sea to make its landfall over Morayshire.

courses were provided to meet specific needs, such as the Instrument Rating Examiners course, running as and when required.

At RAF Lossiemouth the unit had been instrumental in the training of all *ab initio* Jaguar personnel from the four export countries that currently operate the BAE produced aircraft – Oman, Ecuador, India, and Nigeria – as well as the RAF, and had seen former pupils from these air forces returning to take advantage of the QWI course, experience that cannot be gained elsewhere.

Having provided aircraft and crews for both Operation Desert Shield and later Desert Storm, No.16 Squadron has quite rightly made a place for itself in the history books.

Although a non-operational squadron in peacetime, the JOCU sent crews and aircraft to serve during the Gulf War, as it would do under any national emergency. Equally, the 'staff' or instructors were to maintain their operational expertise, just in case a situation arose whereby the squadron would need to be released from its reserve commitment and become integrated once again into the RAF's front line structure.

No.16 (Reserve) Squadron, when at RAF Lossiemouth, numbered just nine QFIs, along with two flight commanders and the squadron boss. At that period there were generally four students undertaking the long course. This began with two and a half weeks of ground school followed by three dual-handling and one solo-handling sortie. There were five instrument flights, of which four were dual with a instructor and one solo, three sorties involving formation flying, of which two were with the instructor in a Jaguar T.2A, and a package of five trips of low-level flying bringing the general aircraft handling stage to its conclusion.

The weapons phase was built around fifteen sorties, five of which were flown dual, which then lead to simulated attack profiles (SAPs) that were divided into three trips flown as a single ship, the first being dual, and five as part of a formation, which again saw just one flown with an instructor.

Before the students' introduction into the world of air combat (three sorties), and evasion tactics (nine dual sorties), they underwent a number of 'check rides' carried out by a flight commander or the squadron boss. In these, they were assessed on their instrument flying, which led to them achieving an instrument rating and their general handling abilities.

Running parallel to the long course were the short courses of anything from one to five pilots generally tailored to the individual needs of those concerned. Most of the students undertaking a short course were pilots either returning to operational flying or taking over supervisory positions within the squadron structure, for example Flight Commanders.

One of the most important, and quite possibly most demanding, courses run by the squadron were those for Qualified Weapon Instructors. Here pilots selected for the QWI course, which generally caters for up to four students at any one time, were to learn the intricacies of retard bombing, strafing, 'toss ad loft' deliveries, air-to-air firing of both gun and missiles, air combat training (ACT) and tactical management. The course dealt in depth with how the ordnance operates, how best to deliver and its practical application.

Pilots undertaking this course did so at the behest of either their own squadrons, when they were promoted into an executive position or were to become instructors in weaponry in their own right. The instructors of No.16 Squadron were, almost without exception, either QFIs of QWIs.

The QFIs deal with the conversion sorties and the early instrument flying and the QWIs dealt with all the weaponry skills. All other phases including formation, low-level aviation, air combat, simulated attack profiles, evasion training and some of the instrument flying is shared by all the instructors.

The planning of the courses was undertaken at No.1 Group, Strike Command and were dovetailed to maximize the time and resources available. The QWI course, of which there was one each year, was open to

Morayshire is relatively uninhabited and is often referred to by RAF crews as 'moon country'. Here, XX832 turns hard over the winter heather, a landscape representative of much of the terrain on the eastern side of northern Scotland.

other Jaguar users, time being bought from the unit by the country concerned, although with the limited assets currently available this was at times be at the expense of a RAF slot.

When No.16 (Reserve) Squadron disbanded in March 2005 some 1,038 students had passed through the Jaguar training programme of which 841 were new pilots converting onto the aircraft for the first time. Additionally to this a number of instructor pilots were trained by the British Aircraft Corporation (BAC) to provide the initial core for the JOCU.

Air Commodore Graham Wright who wrote the forward to this book was to pass through its doors no less than four times between ab initio conversion to becoming station commander at RAF Coltishall. Fl. Lt Matt D'Aubyn who was to become the very last pilot to be trained to fly the Jaguar in the United Kingdom undertook the bulk of his training with No.41 (F) Squadron who had absorbed the final

training course from the disbanding No.16 (Reserve) Squadron to form the Jaguar Training Flight. In an interview given upon graduation he said:

It has only been over the last few days that has made me realize the historic significance of being the last pilot to be trained on the aircraft. Whilst I knew that I was in fact the last pilot to convert to the Jaguar, my focus was totally towards graduating from the Jaguar Training Flight.

It is now that I realised that I am the last of over 800 pilots to be trained on the Jaguar – an honour indeed.

Graham Wright, then a group captain and Coltishall's station commander, said:

The graduation of Matt D'Aubyn as the last Jaguar pilot to be trained on the aircraft, despite the fact that it has been planned for some time, forces home the realization that the end of an era has dawned on the Jaguar fraternity.

Since my initial training on the Jaguar with 226 OCU at RAF Lossiemouth in 1985, I have undertaken refresher courses as a flight commander, squadron commander and most recently as preparation to take command of RAF Coltishall, and this continued contact with the OCU is typical of all of us who have served on the Jaguar Force.

Indeed it is sobering to think that every Jaguar pilot has passed through that unit in its various forms as JOCU, 226 OCU, 16 [®] Squadron and finally as the Jaguar Training Flight. The OCU therefore has a great history of its own and everybody involved in the Jaguar training process over the years should be immensely proud of their achievements.

Aberdeenshire is in quite striking contrast to the heather-covered terrain of Morayshire. Undulating and green, it provides some fine scenery while also providing a demanding flying environment.

Low cloud and undulating countryside can create its own hazards during a let-down. Here XZ108, skimming through the layers, looks for a suitable opening to enter the low level.

Venting fuel as the pair of Jaguars begin to climb, while the landscape provides a mixture of winter shades.

Northern Scotland, apart from providing a superb training environment with minimum disruption to local inhabitants, also creates some very pleasing backdrops for the photographer. Here XZ108 and XX832 skirt over a causeway with the North Sea beckoning in the background.

Left Fully aerobatic, the Jaguar T.2 of No.16 (Reserve) Squadron rolls off the top of a loop, providing the photographer with one of the more dramatic poses.

Below Jaguar GR.1A XZ108 'A' No.16 (Reserve) Squadron was initially assigned to No.II (AC) Squadron. The jet subsequently had a chequered career, suffering a landing mishap at De Peel in 1978 and then, more dramatically, colliding with a Tornado in January 1990. On that occasion the Tornado crashed, with the crew ejecting safely. XZ108 recovered to RAF Leeming with 1m of wing missing. It finally met its end on 3 September 1998, when it crashed off the Norfolk coast.

In a standard training fit of two external tanks and a pair of CBLS practice bomb dispensers, Jaguar GR.1A XZ108 creates a striking pose as it goes vertical.

With rain squalls in the background, the winter sun creates a pleasing rainbow as a backdrop to the Jaguar as it passes over the Morayshire heather.

Dive-bombing can be a very hazardous form of ordnance delivery, with airspeed building up rapidly and the hard deck coming up at an equally frightening rate. Such was the Jaguar's NAVWASS and later FIN 1064, that much of the risk was eliminated, although target fixation could still be a major problem if not managed correctly.

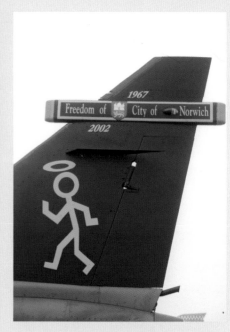

Above No.16 (Reserve) Squadron relocated to RAF Coltishall in July 2000, bringing all remaining Jaguar operators under one roof, fittingly to the main home of the Jaguar. In 2002, the station was granted the freedom of the City of Norwich and the markings of the 2002 display aircraft were altered to represent this.

Below The squadron's ninetieth anniversary in 2005 also brought forth a tastefully decorated fin on XX117.

Turning for home, XZ108 'A', wearing the pennant of Wing Commander Brian Newby, and T.2 XX832 'Z' turn for RAF Lossiemouth following a sortie on 23 November 1995.

Throughout its tenure at RAF Coltishall, No.16 (Reserve) Squadron continued to provide the Jaguar solo display for the RAF, although the specially marked aircraft, XX766, assigned the code 'PE', still took its place in the general pool of aircraft.

The relocation saw the squadron's aircraft adopt the now standard two-letter code for its aircraft. Here, Jaguar GR.3 XZ115 'PD' can be seen formating late one afternoon in December 2003 on a Tristar KC.1 of No.216 Squadron.

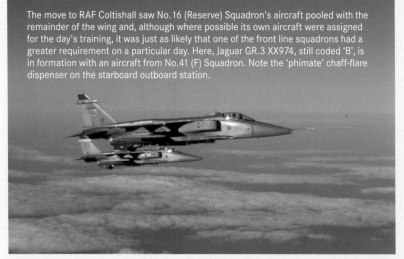

The move to RAF Coltishall saw No.16 (Reserve) Squadron's aircraft pooled with the remainder of the wing and, although where possible its own aircraft were assigned for the day's training, it was just as likely that one of the front line squadrons had a greater requirement on a particular day. Here, Jaguar GR.3 XX974, still coded 'B', is in formation with an aircraft from No.41 (F) Squadron. Note the 'phimate' chaff-flare dispenser on the starboard outboard station.

Jaguar T.4 XX847 'PY' of No.16 (Reserve) Squadron, upgraded in 2001. Earlier in its career it served with 226 OCU, II (AC), 6, 14, 20, 31 and 41 Squadrons. It also had the distinction of being the 100th Jaguar to undergo overhaul with the Jaguar Maintenance Unit at RAF Abingdon in July 1980.

Although technically on the strength of No. 16 (Reserve) Squadron, Jaguar T.4 XX150, seen here, was being operated by No. 6 Squadron when they deployed to the Bulgarian Air Base at Graf Ignatievo to operate alongside the MiG–21bis 'Fishbed L' and Su25K 'Frogfoot' of the Bulgarski Voenno Vazdushni Sili (BVVS). The exercise, named Lonecat 02, was to test the very nature of one of NATO's Rapid Reaction Force elements.

After spending over ten years in deep storage at RAF Shawbury, XZ392, seen here landing at the BVVS base of Graf Ignatievo during Exercise Lonecat 02, was upgraded to Jaguar GR.3A configuration and re-issued to No.16 (Reserve) Squadron on 26 March 2003. The jet joined seven other aircraft to operate with No.6 Squadron when it became the first NATO-assigned fighter unit to operate in Bulgaria.

Passing over the town of Peterhead, these two Jaguars have coasted in prior to entering the low level. Pictured in November 1995 when No. 16 (Reserve) Squadron was still stationed at RAF Lossiemouth, the Jaguars that operate from Coningsby today still find this area among the most suitable for their training.

RAF COLTISHALL

Of all the stations to have operated the Jaguar, RAF Coltishall, although not the first, will always be considered the home of the Jaguar.

Planned as a bomber station, the construction of Royal Air Force Coltishall began in February 1939, but it was pressed into use as a fighter station in May 1940 while still incomplete. It has remained continuously in use as a fighter station to this day. This long association with air defence is commemorated in the station badge and its motto – 'Aggressive in Defence'.

Coltishall is one of the last surviving Battle of Britain front line fighter stations, the other being RAF Northolt, and, when it finally closes at the end of October 2006, it will have been at the heart of the UK defence structure continuously for sixty-six years. For over half of that it will have been home to the Jaguar, and it is perhaps a travesty that the loss of both do not go hand in hand.

The history surrounding Coltishall is one of unsurpassed glory from that day on 29 May 1940 when RAF Coltishall welcomed its first squadron. Under the command of Squadron Leader Rupert Leigh, No.66 Squadron, with their Spitfire Mk 1s, moved the short distance from another Norfolk airfield at RAF Watton. They were joined three days later by No.242 Squadron, a Hurricane squadron manned mainly by Canadian pilots who had joined the Royal Air Force prior to the start of the war. Coinciding with their arrival at RAF Coltishall was the appointment of a new squadron commander, a thirty-year-old fighter pilot with artificial legs – Squadron Leader Douglas Bader.

RAF Coltishall was declared fully operational to No.12 Group (Fighter Command) at 00.01 hrs on 23 June 1940 by the station commander, Wing Commander W.K. Beisiegal.

The first recorded kill of the Battle of Britain is credited to No.66 Squadron. Following a 04.40 hrs take-off, Sergeant F.N. Robertson, flying his Spitfire Mk 1 (aircraft N3035), and accompanied by two other Spitfires, climbed to 15,000ft and intercepted a lone Dornier 17 bomber in the skies over Winterton. The gunner of the enemy aircraft successfully hit one of the Spitfires, forcing him to return to base. The remaining pair continued the assault until Sergeant Robertson mortally wounded the Dornier that crashed into the sea. As the battle progressed, the station was used as a base for resting squadrons from No.11 Group in south-east England, but

Royal Air Force Coltishall must be considered the home of the Jaguar, for although the Jaguar first operated from Lossiemouth, it was Coltishall that was to be home for three front line squadrons for over thirty years. The station itself celebrated its sixty-fifth anniversary in 2005 and, to mark that event, aircraft XZ112 received a special tail scheme. It is depicted here alongside that of the No.41 (F) Squadron display mount for the 2005 display season.

the station's own squadrons played an aggressive part, belonging to the celebrated 'Duxford Wing' and destroying a total of eighty enemy aircraft. Famous 'aces' such as Stanford Tuck, 'Sailor' Malan, 'Cat's Eyes' Cunningham and Johnnie Johnson all flew from the base during the Second World War.

On 8 August 1945 RAF Coltishall was handed over to the Polish Air Force and became RAF Coltishall (Polish) under the command of Group Captain T.H. Polski. This change was to see the transfer of personnel from No.133 Polish Wing HQ, Squadron Nos 306, 309 and 315, as well as (Polish) Servicing Echelons Nos 6306, 6309, and 6315. The station was handed back to RAF Fighter Command in February 1946.

Early in 1957 a contract was let to extend the runway and to strengthen both the runway and taxiways. During this period the aircraft were moved to RAF Horsham St Faith near Norwich. While on this detachment both Coltishall squadrons began to re-equip with the Javelin FAW 4 aircraft, and in doing so became the first Javelin Wing in Fighter Command.

The year 1958 saw extensive alterations to the station, in preparation for the arrival of the Air Fighter Development Squadron (AFDS) of the Central Fighter Establishment (CFE) and the very first Lightnings in RAF service. The first of the pre-production aircraft to be delivered was XG334/A, which arrived at Coltishall on 23 December 1959, followed by XG335/B and XG336/C a few days after Christmas. Towards the end of 1959, Coltishall's resident Hunter unit, No.74 Squadron, was informed that they were to be the first front line operational squadron in the RAF to be equipped with the Mach 2-capable English Electric Lightning. The squadron became operational on 29 June 1960.

From 13 April 1964 to 30 September 1974, Coltishall was the home of No.226 Operational Conversion Unit. Its role was to train pilots to fly the Mach 2 Lightning interceptor. Prior to the disbandment of the OCU in 1974, 810 pilots had been trained to fly this mighty aircraft.

In April 1963 Coltishall became the home of the Historic Aircraft Flight, which would later become the Battle of Britain Memorial Flight. As the last of the Lightnings left the base in 1974 to be replaced by the Anglo–French Jaguar, it became obvious that more space was needed at Coltishall and, therefore, in 1976 the decision was made to relocate the Battle of Britain Memorial Flight to Coningsby in Lincolnshire. In an emotional send-off, 7,000 local people gathered to bid farewell to these historic aircraft.

The first Jaguar squadron at RAF Coltishall was No.54 (Fighter) Squadron, arriving on 8 August 1974 from Coningsby under the command of Wing Commander Terry Carlton.

Wing Commander John Quarterman then led No.6 Squadron south from RAF Lossiemouth in November 1974, from where it had also re-equipped with the Jaguar. No. 41 (F) Squadron arrived at Coltishall in April 1977. This squadron, like both Squadron Nos 6 and 54, was converted from the Phantom FGR.2, and had also been based at Coningsby. The first Jaguars to visit RAF Coltishall, however, had done so several months earlier, when GR.1 XX723 and T.2 XX137 both visited from Lossiemouth on 13

May 1974. The first recorded overshoot had pre-dated these by several months, with XX116 from Warton undertaking an approach on 12 September 1973, and XX109, in company with the ill-fated XX136, doing the same on 27 September while operating from Boscombe Down.

Until 1990, sixteen years after its arrival, the Jaguar was never used in anger. However, the Iraqi invasion of Kuwait changed this situation. Once the backbone of the RAF Ground Attack Force, the Jaguar had largely been replaced by the Tornado GR.1. Despite their age, Jaguars could offer vital low-level ground attack capability as 'Tank Busters' should the Iraqi army advance into Saudi Arabia.

As the situation progressed RAF Coltishall assembled a composite squadron, together with 300 personnel to support them. The desert camouflage paint arrived at the station shortly before midnight the day before the Jaguars' departure. It was all hands to the pumps, including the employment of Air Training Corps cadets on summer camp. Their achievement was superb: ten aircraft were re-painted in full desert camouflage in less than five hours.

With the drawdown of the Jaguar Force and RAF Coltishall, Squadron Nos 54 (F) and 16 (R) disbanded on 11 March 2005. No.41 (F) Squadron would disband in March 2006 and, at the same time, No.6 Squadron would re-locate to RAF Coningsby. The station itself continues to support Jaguar operations through the retention of the Jaguar simulator and the engine test cell.

The sixtieth anniversary of the base was similarly celebrated and, at that time, Jaguar GR.3 XZ364 was to receive a celebratory scheme. It is seen here high over the North Sea fitted with the Vinten JRRP and over-wing missile rails.

No.6 Squadron

No.6 (Designate) Squadron formed at RAF Lossiemouth with the Jaguar GR.1 in September 1974 some six months after its sister squadron, No.54. At RAF Coningsby, the squadron continued to operate the Phantom FGR.2 and, upon standing down on 30 September, it allowed the unit at Lossiemouth to take on the full mantle the following day. The former mounts were re-assigned to No.29 Squadron in the air defence role that had been relinquished by the EE Lightning F.3.

Transfer to RAF Coltishall followed just over a month later when, on 6 November, the squadron arrived at its new home, bringing with it seven aircraft: XX727, 730, 734, 735, 738, 740 and T.2 XX150. Unlike those of No.54 (F) Squadron, these incorporated all the latest modifications, the most obvious of which was the re-designed nose profile to house the laser rangefinder. The arrival at Coltishall was the start of an association that was to last over thirty years, by the end of which the station was truly considered the Jaguar's home.

No.6 Squadron has the longest continuous history of any RAF squadron. It is the only one of the original seven RFC squadrons never to have been disbanded or reduced to a cadre. The squadron has been on operational service longer than any other RAF squadron, and most of its time has been spent overseas, mainly in the Middle and Near East.

No.6 Squadron was the second RAF squadron to operate the Jaguar and the second to take up residence at Coltishall. In this shot, taken in October 1977, ironically at RAF Lossiemouth, is the third production Jaguar GR.1, XX110, in the colours of No.6 Squadron. By this time the jet had been retro-fitted with the LRMTS nose, an in-flight refuelling probe, and had received the all-over wrap-around camouflage scheme.

With a full load of inert 1000lb bombs, XX110 lines up as the No.3 aircraft of a four ship package en route to a range area during a Mallet Blow exercise.

No.6 was formed at Farnborough on 31 January 1914 under the command of Captain J.H.W. Becke. The First World War broke out only seven months later and the squadron crossed to France on 9 September 1914. Like all the RFC squadrons of the time, No.6 Squadron was mainly concerned with army co-operation but was very versatile. The squadron's first air-to-air victory soon occurred when Captain A.C.E. Marsh, while on a bombing raid, captured a German aircraft near St Omer. By the end of 1914, the squadron had become a fully developed army co-operation squadron; its duties including tactical reconnaissance, artillery observation, photography and trench mapping.

Early in 1915, No.6 Squadron started to fly 'scouts' to provide fighter defence for the army co-operation aircraft against German air attacks, which were becoming increasingly frequent. On 25 July 1915, one of the squadron pilots, Captain L.G. Hawker, flying a Bristol Scout, attacked three German aircraft in quick succession and shot the third down in flames. For this exploit, Captain Hawker was awarded the Victoria Cross, the first to be awarded for air-to-air fighting.

After the First World War, the squadron was to serve almost continuously overseas, mainly in the Middle and Near East. When the Second World War commenced, it was ideally placed to support operations in the western desert where, in 1942, when equipped with Hawker Hurricane Mk IIDs, the squadron became so successful at 'tank busting', using the under-wing 40mm cannon, that they gained the name 'The Flying Can Openers'. The can-opener emblem is still carried by the squadron aircraft, in addition to the squadron badge.

The squadron returned to the Middle East immediately after cessation of hostilities and had moved to Cyprus in 1956, flying Venoms in attacks on Egyptian airfields during the Suez Crisis. In 1957, the squadron re-equipped with Canberras but remained in Cyprus. In 1969, it returned to the United Kingdom for the first time since 1914 to be based at Coningsby and fly the Phantom in the ground-attack role. In 1974, the squadron re-equipped with Jaguar GR.1 and T.2 aircraft, initially forming at RAF Lossiemouth before moving to Coltishall.

In the sixteen years leading up to the end of the Cold War, the warming of East–West relations saw No.6 Squadron and its two sister squadrons conducting the standard round of exercises and detachments to enhance training and operational capability. In 1979, with the impending export of Jaguar to India, the squadron was to give up seven of its mounts for interim loan with 54 Squadron providing two and 226 OCU four. Most of these aircraft were on overhaul with the JMU at RAF Abingdon or already with BAE SYSTEMS at Warton. The squadron in turn was to receive fresh aircraft from the pool of reserves that were already in the system.

No.6 was the first RAF squadron to deploy forward, back to the desert, for Operation Desert Shield, and several squadron pilots earned individual battle honours flying bombing missions into Kuwait during Operation Desert Storm, the Gulf War of 1991.

The squadron has continued to contribute to world peace with frequent detachments to live theatres of operations. In 1992 and 1993, the squadron was involved in Operation Warden flying Jaguar reconnaissance missions over the north of Iraq in support of the United Nations (UN) peacekeeping efforts on behalf of the Kurdish people. Many of these missions over-flew the airfields that had once been havens to the squadron.

In July 1993 the squadron returned to another old haunt, at Gioia del Colle, near Taranto in Italy, engaged on another UN mission – Operation Deny Flight – providing airborne support for UN Protection Forces in Bosnia. Under the UK designation of 'Operation Grapple' the squadron took with them twelve aircraft in the shape of XZ109/EN, XZ118/FF, XX970/EH, XZ113/FD, XZ112/GA, XZ373/GF, XZ114/FB, XZ104/FM, XZ362/GC, XZ394/

GN, XZ356/EP and XX974/GH. In this year the squadron also celebrated eighty years of unbroken RAF service. The celebrations included a visit by HRH Prince Faisal of Jordan, re-establishing the squadron's longstanding links with the Middle East.

On 30 August 1995 the squadron were the first to use the TIALD/Jaguar GR.1B combination in anger, designating targets for LGB-carrying Harrier GR.7s of No.IV(AC) Squadron during Operation Deliberate Forge, and in the process demonstrating better accuracy than had been achieved by USAF F-111Fs and F-117s during the Gulf War.

No.6 Squadron undertook five such deployments to Italy in support of Operation Deny Flight and were the final Jaguar squadron to undertake this mission, fittingly notching up the 5,000th hour of Jaguar operational flying over the former Yugoslavia. On the squadron's return to Coltishall, it was the first time in three years that all three squadrons had been in residence at the station at the same time, apart from a brief period in 1991 immediately after Operation Desert Storm.

The squadron returned to Gioia Del Colle in June 1997, to provide support to the NATO Stabilisation Force (SFOR) in Bosnia as part of Operation Deliberate Guard, while Coltishall Jaguars were again in Italy during June 1998 as part of Operation Determined Falcon.

Landing at Coltishall in clean configuration is XX970 'EH'. The aircraft had just returned from a very short ACM sortie over the North Sea and is perhaps fairly unique in the Jaguar world in that it has served with No.6 Squadron for over twenty years, initially as a Jaguar GR.1A, then as a GR.1A(T) or GR.1B, and finally as a GR.3A. In that time it has supported operations in the desert, Turkey and Kosovo, sporting a number of differing schemes.

The seventy-fifth anniversary of No.6 Squadron prompted the above scheme. Not a patch on today's themes but in 1989 it was perhaps considered appropriate. It was certainly tastefully designed with a full-sized squadron crest on the fin.

In August 2002 the squadron deployed six single-seat Jaguar GR.3/3A aircraft and a pair of twin-seat Jaguar T.2As to the Bulgarian base at Graf Ignatievo just to the south of Plovdiv as part of Exercise LoneCat 02, and became the first RAF fast jet squadron to operate with the Bulgarski Voenno-Vazdushni (BVVS) since the end of the Cold War. This was followed in September 2004 by a visit to Constanta air base in Romania for Exercise Lone Cheetah. It remains the last operational front line Jaguar squadron in the RAF.

Motto: *Oculi Exercitus* ('The Eyes of the Army')

Above Air-to-air refuelling is a bread and butter task for the Jaguar in its role as part of NATO's Rapid Reaction Force. Here, three jets formate on Tristar K.1 ZD951 of No.216 Squadron.

Left In 1993 a number of aircraft received the 'Flying Can Openers' inscription on the fin, including XX962 'EK', which had served in the Gulf with the 'Fat Slags' nose art.

Below Another of the Gulf aircraft was XZ358, named 'Diplomatic Service'. This jet undertook six attack missions, where it dropped a total of eighteen 1,000lb bombs, two missions where six cluster bomb units were used, and six reconnaissance missions.

Below The Gulf War and Operation Granby breathed new life into the Jaguar, during which period it became an indispensable asset. No.6 Squadron, along with the rest of the Coltishall wing, supported operations following Iraq's invasion of Kuwait. This particular aircraft, XZ356, was drawn from the squadron's establishment to be part of the composite squadron in theatre. Originally a 'spare' aircraft for the initial deployment it was later to receive the so-called 'Gulf mods' and then flown to Thumrait as a replacement. Named 'Mary Rose' it undertook thirty-three missions during the war.

During the mid-1990s, following a number of high profile mid-air collisions or near collisions, the RAF, along with some of its NATO partners, was prompted to experiment with various colourful options to make the jets easier to see in the peacetime environment. Tornado, Harrier and Phantom units opted for brightly coloured red, white or blue tails. At Coltishall a trial was carried out using white external tanks. Two aircraft were assigned to these tests, including XZ399 'EL', depicted here in formation with No.54 (F) Squadron's XX767 'GE'.

Breaking hard, Jaguar T.2A XX141 'EV' of No.6 Squadron peels away to drop into the low level.

Thirteen Jaguar GR.1As were to receive modifications to be in a position to carry TIALD. The aircraft chosen had all received the 'stage three' upgrade that included provision for over-wing missile rails and Sky Guardian RWR. The first three jets equipped to carry TIALD were XZ381, XX962 and XX748. Unofficially designated GR.1B and later GR.1A(T), even when the Deny Flight tasking was handed over to the Harrier GR.7, Jaguars were still called upon to provide designation. Seen here landing at Gioia del Colle on 20 August 1995 during Operation Deliberate Force with the TIALD pod on the centre-line station is XX962 'EK'.

In their role as part of NATO's Rapid Reaction Force, the Coltishall Jaguars have visited and played host to a number of different air forces. Here 'EQ' of No.6 Squadron taxis out with a Sukhoi Su22M4 of 7 Elt Polish Air Force for company.

The year 1998 saw the twenty-fifth anniversary of the entry of the Jaguar into front line service. A celebratory event was held over the weekend of 1 to 3 October and this No.6 Squadron aircraft, XZ396, received a commemorative tail marking. The aircraft, one of the last to be delivered to the RAF, has served its entire career with No.6 Squadron, with whom it is still current today.

No.6 Squadron lined up at the BVVS base of Graf Ignatievo during Exercise Lonecat 02.

The 'medium altitude' ARTF scheme was very much a temporary affair, becoming very scruffy in a relatively short space of time. Here XX737 'EE' of No.6 Squadron reveals its normal grey scheme beneath.

Left Jaguar GR.3 XX116 'EO' of No.6 Squadron waits at the last chance before departing on a live weapon sortie from RAF Coltishall. The jet has a single 2,000lb bomb on the centre-line station.

Right No.6 Squadron celebrated its ninetieth anniversary in 2004 and, to commemorate the event aircraft, XX110 was given this attractive fin marking. As a trial, however, the marks were applied initially to XZ367, which acts as the station's weapon load trainer.

No.41 Squadron

No.41 (F) Squadron was the third of the Coltishall squadrons to equip with the Jaguar GR.1 and, unlike its two sister squadrons, was tasked with a dual role of tactical reconnaissance and ground attack.

On 1 October 1976, No.41 (Designate) Squadron was formed at RAF Coltishall with Jaguar GR.1 aircraft, and for six months the two squadrons operated independently. In April 1977 the Phantom squadron was disbanded, the standard was handed over to the Jaguar squadron, and the 'Designate' caveat was abandoned when the squadron was declared combat-ready in a reconnaissance role, a role it has subsequently retained.

In February 1978 the squadron became part of SACEUR's Strategic Reserve (Air) and in 1983 was assigned to the Allied Command Europe Mobile Force (AMF) both involving regular deployments to northern Norway, operating from the often snow-covered runway at Bardufoss. To support the reconnaissance role, the squadron had a Reconnaissance Intelligence Centre (RIC) that was responsible for the processing and interpretation of photographs taken by the aircraft. The RIC at Coltishall was a permanent building but air-portable versions of the facility were used for the off-base deployments. A typical reconnaissance mission is flown at 250ft and the dispatch standard for the mission results is forty-five minutes between engines off and delivery of photographs/reports to the tasking agency.

Like its sister squadrons, No.41 (F) Squadron has an illustrious service history. It was formed as part of the Royal Flying Corps at Gosport on 14 July 1916, almost two years before the Royal Air Force was formed. Equipped initially with FE8 fighters, the squadron was posted to St Omer, France, on the Western Front in October 1916. Until the end of the First World War the squadron served continuously in France and Belgium, successively re-equipping with SE5 and DH5 aircraft and mainly engaged in offensive patrolling, escort duties and later low-level reconnaissance and ground attack. By the end of the war the squadron was credited with 124 enemy aircraft destroyed, 112 probable, plus the destruction of nineteen hostile kite balloons. The people of St Omer later honoured the squadron by granting permission for the double-armed cross, which is a feature of the arms of St Omer, to be incorporated into the squadron badge.

Between the end of the First World War and the arrival of the jet age the squadron followed a similar history pattern to many of it contemporaries. During the Abyssinian crisis, from October 1935 to August 1936, No.41 (F) Squadron was to serve in the Western Aden Protectorate. During the evacuation of Dunkirk and the Battle of Britain, the squadron logged over 100 combat victories. Equipped with the Vickers Supermarine Spitfire it was one of the few units that flew the famous fighter for the whole of the conflict, receiving improved models as they became available.

During the Second World War, No.41 (F) Squadron was credited with destroying 200 enemy aircraft, probably destroyed a further sixty-one, and damaged 109.

Passing on to more advanced piston-powered types, and eventually into the jet age, the squadron stayed at the front of the RAF's day fighter force. It was on 1 February 1958 that No.41 (F) Squadron was reconstituted at RAF Coltishall, changing from a day fighter role to a night, all-weather unit. In doing so it absorbed the personnel and Javelins of No.141 Squadron, which had been de-activated the previous day. In July 1958 the squadron moved to RAF Wattisham, where it remained until disbanding on 31 December 1963. Two years later, in September 1965, No.41 (F) Squadron re-formed at RAF West Raynham as a Fighter Command surface-to-air missile squadron equipped with Bloodhound Mk 2

By July 1984 the markings on No.41's jets had been revised further, with the addition of the fin band. Pictured here is XZ363 'A'.

missiles. The squadron was again disbanded on 18 September 1970, the standard being temporarily laid up in the Church of St Michael and St George, RAF West Raynham. On 1 April 1972, No.41 (F) Squadron reformed as a fighter squadron with No.38 Group, Air Support Command, operating Phantom FGR.2 aircraft from Coningsby. It then specialised in tactical fighter reconnaissance with a secondary role in ground attack.

The arrival of the Jaguar in 1976 saw the squadron receive factory-fresh jets in the serial range XZ113–XZ119 and XZ355–XZ360, following on immediately from those assigned to No.II (AC) Squadron in Germany. The bulk of these, because of their specialised reconnaissance role and ability to carry and operate the BAC-built reconnaissance pod, were to remain on squadron strength until the advent of the newer and much smaller 'Jaguar Replacement Reconnaissance Pod' (JRRP) in the 1990s. Ironically, the BAE SYSTEMS 2000 infra-red line-scan reconnaissance package, TIRRS, designed for the Tornado GR.1A to replace the 'old' podded system of the Jaguar, was itself down-declared in 2004. Its task, or part of it, was assigned to 'JRP' (having been re-designated 'Joint Reconnaissance Pod' by this time).

No.41 (F) Squadron took part in Operation Desert Storm, and, as part of the coalition air force, conducted numerous reconnaissance and bombing sorties against Iraqi forces in support of the liberation of Kuwait. As part of Operation Desert Shield the squadron departed the UK for Thumrait, Oman, on 11 August 1990, taking with it twelve aircraft in four flights of three, comprising XZ363, XX974, XX112, XX719, XZ396, XX970, XZ357, XZ115, XZ355, XZ372, XX741 and XZ369, all sporting the desert pink ARTF scheme. These were to return to the UK by 11 November, having been replaced in theatre by aircraft with uprated engines and the provision for over-wing missile rails. The twelve fresh aircraft departed Coltishall in two batches of seven and five: XX725, XX733, XZ119, XZ358, XZ364, XZ367 and XZ375 on 23 October, and XX748, XX754, XX962, XZ118 and XZ356 on 2 November, with Muharraq, Bahrain, as their ultimate destination.

As a result of the war, after returning from the Gulf, the Jaguar wing deployed to Incirlik, in south-west Turkey, to participate in Operation Warden, providing an air presence necessary to secure a safe haven for the Kurdish people of northern Iraq. This commitment was handed over to the Harriers in April 1993, to be replaced less than four months later by a similar role in support of Operation Deny Flight or, in RAF parlance, 'Operation Grapple', policing the skies above the Bosnian conflict from a base in southern Italy. Twelve aircraft were to deploy to Gioia del Colle, Italy, on 16 July 1993, comprising XZ109/EN, XZ118/FF, XX970/EH, XZ113/FD, XZ112/GA, XZ373/GF, XZ114/FB, XZ104/FM, XZ362/GC, XZ394/GN, XZ356/EP, all sporting the grey (baby blue) ARTF paint scheme. It was during this period of operations that a 41 (F) Jaguar became the first RAF aircraft to drop a bomb in anger over Europe since 1945. This attack was carried out against a Bosnian Serb tank, and resulted in the tank being severely damaged.

The Jaguar Wing handed over responsibility for the UN-controlled Operation Deny Flight to the Harrier Force in August 1995, and enjoyed a well earned break from operations. However, only a matter of weeks later, 41 (F) Squadron were tasked to return to Gioia del Colle to laser-designate for the Harriers undertaking sorties in support of Operation Deliberate Force, utilising two (XX725 and XX748) of the twelve aircraft eventually modified to operate TIALD. On 1 January 1996, 41 (F) Squadron was declared, along with the rest of the Jaguar Wing, an asset to NATO's Rapid Reaction Force, ready to deploy at short notice in support of NATO operations anywhere within the sphere of NATO's influence.

This call was not long in coming, and the Jaguars were re-summoned to Gioia del Colle in February 1996 in support of Operation Deliberate Guard with No.41 (F) Squadron becoming the lead squadron. The Jaguars were to return to Italy yet again on 13 June 1998 for Operation Determined Falcon. They returned home on 2 July 1998, before another recall, this time for Operation Warden, in September 1998. They took with them aircraft XZ107/FH, XZ115/FC, XZ118/PF and XZ367/GP.

During 2005 the squadron provided the Jaguar solo display for the RAF and, upon the demise of 16 (Reserve) Squadron, added an additional flight to its establishment to bridge the gap in type conversion for the last 'new' Jaguar pilot and those returning to the aircraft from other duties. This ended following the graduation of the RAF's last Jaguar pilot, Fl. Lt Matt D'Aubyn, on 10 October 2005. The squadron itself disbanded at the end of March 2006, handing its mantle and standard on to the Fast Jet and Weapon Operational Evaluation Unit (FJ&WOEU) at RAF Coningsby.

No.54 Squadron

No.54 (F) Squadron became the first front line RAF squadron to operate the Sepecat Jaguar GR.1. Formed at RAF Lossiemouth on 29 March 1974, No.54 (Designate) Squadron operated in parallel to No.54 Squadron, which was still operating the McDonnell Phantom FGR.2 at RAF Coningsby. The latter transferred its mounts to the re-forming No.111 Squadron on 1 July 1974 with

No.54 (F) Squadron then dropping the 'designate' caveat while still at RAF Lossiemouth, before re-locating to its final home at RAF Coltishall on 5 August 1974.

The squadron arrived at the Norfolk base bringing with it eight Jaguar GR.1 aircraft in the shape of XX121, 719, 721–725 and XX732, the bulk of which still retained the original 'French' nose, lacking the LRMTS laser range finder housing. These were to be retro-fitted at a later date.

Coltishall was to be home for the next thirty years, during which time both aircraft and station matured to provide RAF Strike Command with a cutting edge that was the envy of the world.

No.54 (F) Squadron has an envious history born out of humble beginnings. Formed at Castle Bromwich on 15 May 1916, it was equipped with BE.2Cs and AVRO 504s. Initially responsible for Home Defence, it soon moved to France, where it was re-equipped with Sopwith Scouts and played a distinguished part in the fighting on the Western Front, gaining battle honours at Arras, Merrines, Ypres and Cambrai. In December 1917, the squadron received Sopwith Camels and first began operating in the ground attack role in support of the Fifth Army. It distinguished itself in co-operation with the ground forces and took part in the defence of Chateau Thierry. At the end of the war the squadron was disbanded at Yatesbury in October 1919, to re-form again at Hornchurch in January 1930.

No.54 (F) Squadron was the first front line RAF squadron to convert to the Sepecat Jaguar. The squadron received six aircraft with the 'French nose', which lacked provision for LRMTS – XX719 and XX721–725 – although these were later retro-fitted. Here XX719 is seen shortly after its arrival at RAF Coltishall.

Above During its time with No.54 (F) Squadron, XX732 participated in the biennial Bulls Eye exercise held at Husum Air Base in northern Germany during 1979, where it received an attractive 'shark's mouth' marking.

Another of No.54 (F) Squadron's original mounts, XX724, seen at Coltishall in January 1983 during a Mallet Blow exercise. Apart from a period in store at RAF Shawbury, the jet served with the squadron for its entire career of Jaguar operation, in the process being upgraded to GR.1A, GR.3 and finally GR.3A.

During the interwar years it was equipped with Siskin IIIs, Bulldogs, Gauntlets and Gladiators, the last being replaced by Spitfires in 1938 when the squadron role reverted to air defence.

The squadron was still based at Hornchurch at the outbreak of the war, went into the Battle of Britain equipped with Spitfire 1s, and was the top-scoring RAF squadron, with ninety-two kills, thirty-seven of which were shot down on 24 May 1940. After a short 'rest' period at Catterick, the squadron returned to Hornchurch with Spitfire Mk Vs to carry out convoy escort duties, and on 30 March 1941 moved to Rochford Aerodrome, Southend-on-Sea. They gained their 100th kill on 17 April, while operating from that airfield.

In August 1942 the squadron moved to Richmond, Australia, and then to Darwin, where it re-equipped with the Spitfire Vc and later the Spitfire Mk XIII. Here it stayed for the rest of the war, where it saw sporadic action against the withdrawing Japanese forces. It was disbanded in November 1945.

It re-formed immediately at Chilbolton with Tempests and, with the advent of the jet age, moved to Odiham in 1946. Here it flew Vampires, becoming the first squadron to fly them in the night role, and flying the first jet transatlantic flight in 1948.

The squadron progressed from Vampires to Meteors and then to Hunters in 1955, and in 1959 moved to Stradishall where, in March 1960, it became a ground attack squadron once more, operating with Hunter FGA.9s. It moved again in 1961 to Waterbeach, and in 1962 joined No.1 Squadron to become the Offensive Support Wing of No.38 Group. In this role the squadron flew its first operational sorties for eighteen years during the Yemini/Republican friction on the Aden frontier. In 1963 the squadron moved to West Raynham and was awarded its standard in May of that year.

On 1 September 1969, after fourteen years of Hunter flying, the 54 Squadron badge was taken over by the second RAF Phantom FGR.2 squadron, based at Coningsby. The squadron became operational using the Phantom on 1 January 1970 and, during its time at Coningsby, created a world record during a deployment to the Far East, where it made a non-stop flight from the United Kingdom to Singapore in fourteen hours, eight minutes.

No.54 (F) Squadron, along with its two sister squadrons at RAF Coltishall, followed a fairly standard pattern of exercises and detachments to enhance operating capability during the Cold War period, including participation at the 1979 'Bulls Eye' exercise, held at Husum, West Germany, where two of the squadron's aircraft received highly coloured shark mouths. This was followed by the first 'Red Flag' participation in 1980, and No.54 then became the first Jaguar squadron to receive the avionics upgrade package. The first three aircraft to be upgraded with FIN 1064 were XX733 in September 1983 at Warton, followed by XZ400 in December 1983 and XZ365 in March 1984 at the JMU Abingdon. All three were returned to the squadron although XX733 spent a period on trial at Boscombe Down.

With the break up of the Warsaw Pact, re-unification of the 'two Germanys' and the warming of East–West relations, the outlook for any front line RAF squadron looked changeable. In the case of the Jaguar squadrons already supplanted in the 'strike' role by

One of the few early ex-Germany aircraft to transfer to other front line units. Seen here climbing out from RAF Coltishall, the jet was assigned to No.54 (F) Squadron in October 1985. However, by October 1990 it had passed into store at RAF Shawbury and never returned to front line service. It is now preserved in the German Aerospace Museum at Hermeskeil.

Following service in Germany, XZ392 was transferred to No.54 (F) Squadron during 1984, with whom it served until 1990 when it was placed in store. With relatively few hours on the airframe, it was removed from storage on 8 November 2004 and taken to DARA at St Athan for overhaul and upgrade to Jaguar GR.3A. It returned to front line service on 24 February 2005.

XZ112 has become a Jaguar of many colours. It is seen here in special markings to commemorate No.54 (F) Squadron's seventy-fifth anniversary. The jet was later to receive the '89th Anniversary' scheme and currently displays the RAF Coltishall '65th Anniversary' markings.

the Panavia Tornado, the future looked anything but rosy, with the inevitable defence cuts looming around the corner. Then came the Gulf War of 1991.

Pilots and ground crew from 54 (F) Squadron helped form the twenty-two-strong Jaguar Detachment based at Muharraq in Bahrain. During the three months of the war the detachment flew over 600 war missions without loss.

Soon after the Gulf War 54 (F) Squadron was deployed to Incirlik Air Base in southern Turkey to form part of the Coalition forces patrolling northern Iraq as part of Operation Warden. During the four separate detachments the squadron spent a total of eleven months in Turkey and flew nearly 900 operational sorties over northern Iraq. Only six months after finishing its involvement in Operation Warden the squadron deployed to Gioia del Colle in

Italy in support of Operation Deny Flight, flying more than 200 air patrols over Bosnia. The squadron once again deployed to Gioia del Colle in 1997 on Operation Deliberate Guard with the modified Jaguar 96 aircraft. Later, Operation Radome, Operation Deliberate Guard and Operation Deliberate Force were to be surpassed by Operation Allied Force.

The warming of East–West relations and the growing number of countries interested in joining the NATO alliance presented many opportunities and challenges for Western air forces. The Jaguars at RAF Coltishall were to spearhead many of these initiatives, participating in Exercise Strong Resolve 2002, held at Miroslawice, Poland.

Sadly, as part of the drawdown of the Jaguar Force and RAF Coltishall, No.54 (F) Squadron disbanded on 11 March 2005.

Left The first all-over grey Jaguar for No.54 (F) Squadron was XZ362 'GC', which returned to the unit following painting on 23 January 1996. Six months later, it was lost in a crash in Alaska during a DACT mission during Exercise Cope Thunder.

Below Captured over Norfolk during practice for the 1997 Queen's birthday flypast. XZ108 'GL' had, by this time, been modified to Jaguar 96 (R) configuration, following transfer from No.16 (Reserve) Squadron.

Below One of the first three Jaguars to be equipped to operate TIALD was XX748, seen here taking on fuel from an RAF VC–10 tanker in February 1996. The pastel shades in the RAF roundel are a legacy of operating in an ARTF scheme.

Having seen conversion to Jaguar GR.1A, Jaguar 96, Jaguar 97, and finally re-designated Jaguar GR.3A, XX119 'GD' is one of the oldest RAF Jaguars still flying, having been delivered to 226 OCU on 17 December 1973. It is captured here over the North Sea in May 2005.

Call-sign 'Boxer 1–3' on 27 November 2003, XX119 'GD', XZ115 'PD', and XZ364 'GJ', in perfect formation echelon starboard.

XX725 has one of the more colourful histories of the RAF Jaguar. An original No.54 (F) Squadron mount in 1974, it spent four years on loan to the Indian Air Force before returning to RAF charge and upgrading to GR.1A. Served with distinction in the Gulf during Operation Granby as 'Johnny Fartpants', accumulating an impressive forty-seven missions. After receiving the 'stage three' modifications and TIALD conversion, it participated in Operation Deliberate Force where it notched up a further seven operational sorties. Assigned to the SAOEU on Jaguar operational development in October 1996, it returned to front line use periodically and gained this Arctic camouflage scheme for No.54 (F) Squadron's participation in Exercise Snow Goose at Bardufoss in early 2005.

Above Fuji film brings out the best of colours in the setting sun as Jaguar GR.3 XZ364 'GJ' awaits its turn to refuel over the North Sea.

Left No.54 (F) Squadron disbanded in March 2005, one year short of its ninetieth anniversary. However, to mark the passing of the unit, XZ112 received the brightest of all Jaguar special schemes.

RECCE JAGUAR
Front Line Tactical Reconnaissance

RECONNAISSANCE IS TODAY perhaps the most important task performed by any force in the world, yet it is one that tends to be a secondary task in terms of hardware. History shows that photo-reconnaissance (PR) units have always been a long way down the pecking order in terms of equipment and yet without the facility, numerous operations could never have been contemplated, let alone successfully executed.

The Jaguars of Nos II (AC) and 41 (F) Squadrons were to provide the RAF with that prime tactical reconnaissance role throughout the late 1970s through to the 1990s when other systems and multi-user pods became available. No.II (AC) Squadron was located at RAF Laarbruch in West Germany and provided its essential service for 1 BR Corps. The squadron was equipped with the Jaguar GR.1A and later became the first to receive the reconnaissance version of the Tornado GR.1A at the beginning of 1989. At that time it entered into a completely new concept of photo-reconnaissance. Fitted with infrared sensors, including the BAE 1R Linescan 4000 housed in a ventral blister on the forward fuselage section, which afforded very high quality recording of the scene from horizon to horizon by day and night. Known as TIRRS (Tornado Infra-Red Reconnaissance System) by this means the results of any reconnaissance would be recorded on video tape with such accuracy that enlargements could be made for a more detailed examination eliminating the need for the time-consuming photo processing backup. The recording could also be displayed in the cockpit thus enabling the navigator to produce high quality reporting while still airborne. A second Tornado (PR) unit, No.XIII Squadron, also formed at RAF Honington in a similar role to complete the

Unlike the ARTF schemes applied in the 1990s, those used for the Arctic deployments were somewhat crudely applied, although quite effective. The scheme has also been applied to the reconnaissance pod and external tanks. Fortunately, the paint was water-soluble and was generally washed off shortly after the return to the UK.

Tornado program. Ironically, the development of the 'Jaguar Replacement Reconnaissance Pod' (JRRP) that was to be adapted for carriage by other users and renamed the 'Joint Reconnaissance Pod' (JRP) out saw the effectiveness of the Tornados internal linescan system. TIRRS was down declared in 2004.

Before No.41 (F) Squadron was to receive its first Jaguar, the Bruggen strike wing of Squadron Nos 14, 17, 20 and 31 were to transition to the type, and it was to No.II (AC) Squadron at RAF Laarbruch that the first Recce Jaguar, XZ101, was issued. The Recce Jaguar differs only slightly from the more normal strike aircraft, featuring extra wiring and switches applicable to the specially

designed Reconnaissance Pod operation. The pod itself was derived from one already in operation with the Phantom FGR.2 and began service trials in 1975 with an in-service entry of spring 1976. This timescale can be considered somewhat short, but given the experience gained from that designed for the Phantom, was considered feasible. The urgency was also brought about by the experience gained by the Israeli and Egyptian forces during the war in the Middle East and had underlined the necessity for up-to-date reconnaissance information which could be only gained by aircraft flying faster and lower than before.

The view forward from the rear seat of the Jaguar T.2 is surprisingly good as the Jaguars proceed northwards across the English countryside.

The more standard schemed XZ117 'E' begins its turn into trail behind the waiting VC.10K2 tanker.

The pod, carried on the centre-line station, was produced by British Aerospace at Weybridge and contained a selection of cameras. These were installed in two rotatable drums, the rear one carrying alternative modules to enable the complete scene to be covered from horizon to horizon in low to medium-altitude operations. The cameras in the front rotating drum were two low-oblique across track Vinten F95 Mk.10s with 1.5in F2.8 lenses and a forward-looking oblique F95 Mk.7 camera with a 6in F.28 lens. For low-level sorties the rear camera drum contained two high-oblique across track F95 cameras with 3in F2 lenses, although as an alternative mode a medium-level F126 camera module with a 6in F5.6 lens could be fitted.

To allow the Jaguar to step up its low-level reconnaissance missions to speeds approaching Mach 1, the pod also incorporated the Hawker Siddeley infra-red linescan system (IRLS) and this was fed with all the relevant information stored in the Marconi-Elliot navigation and weapons aiming system (NAVWASS), including height, latitude and longitude and aircraft altitude. Therefore, on each frame, the aircraft's position was printed while a facility existed to allow the pilot to mark a particular area of interest for future reference.

This system was enhanced following MOD 1114, which included the installation of the Ferranti FIN 1064 inertial navigation/attack system – considerably more accurate and reliable that the original Marconi NAVWASS. The modification was carried out on approximately eighty aircraft, both single and twin-seat derivatives, and these were re-designated GR.1A and T.2A respectively in the process.

For its attack role, the Jaguar in 1976 relied primarily on the Hunting BL755 cluster bomb unit (CBU). The BL755 is a weapon designed to give a high kill probability against all kinds of targets, both hard and soft-skinned, normally to be found in the battlefield and immediate tactical areas. To compensate for aiming errors inherent in low-level attack in a high-threat area, the CBU covers the target with bomblets in a pattern that is proportioned to those errors.

The BL755 weighs in the region of 277kg and contains 147 bomblets. The normal configuration in an attack profile would be a 264-gallon centre-line fuel tank, two CBUs on each inboard pylon, an AN/ALQ-101 jamming pod on the port outboard pylon and a Philips-MATRA (Phimat) chaff/flare dispenser on the starboard outer pylon. Upgrades outlined

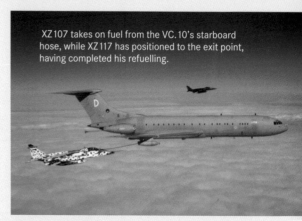

XZ107 takes on fuel from the VC.10's starboard hose, while XZ117 has positioned to the exit point, having completed his refuelling.

elsewhere permitted the Jaguar, as it evolved, to carry more and more precision weapons, reducing the risk of collateral damage and meaning there was less of a need for the use of such indiscriminate weapons as the BL755. Equally, the battle moved steadily from low to medium level as advances in target acquisition and designation improved the kill ratio and, at the same time, increased the delivering platform's survivability.

Breaking into the circuit at RAF Coltishall, the AN/ALE 40 chaff/flare dispenser on the underside of XZ117 can be clearly seen.

To mark the unit's seventy-fifth anniversary in 1991, Jaguar GR.1A XZ398 'A' received the special red fin and spine and is captured here at RAF Lossiemouth during the 1993 tactical fighter meet. The scheme was, by this time, a little scruffy, having been covered by an ARTF finish earlier in the year.

In a newly applied ARTF grey, Jaguar GR.1A XZ357 'FK' is quite striking. A year later, the jet became the first to receive the new permanent grey scheme being adopted by all front line RAF tactical aircraft.

A reconnaissance fit in the 1970s and 1980s would see the Recce-pod, weighing 1,250lb, on the centre-line station, 264-gallon drop tanks on the two inboard stations, with AN/ALQ-101/Phimat as previously described. An option for using the AIM-9L Sidewinder heat-seeking missile for self-protection existed, while located by the engine bay doors in the AN/ALE-40 chaff/flare dispenser. The Recce Jaguar also retained the two nose-mounted internal ADEN 30mm cannon, unlike its Tornado GR.1A cousin. Obviously, the actual configuration would depend on the tactical requirements at the time but, by having and training in a secondary attack role, the squadron remained versatile in the ever-changing scenario.

No.41 (F) Squadron formed part of the ACE Mobile Force (AMF) and was declared to NATO as such. For this role, its deployment area was northern Norway, and in particular Bardufoss, where hardened shelters exist for their use. The squadron's role within the AMF was as a deterrent and as such was used on armed reconnaissance, during which it would be looking for the movement of enemy armour, particularly at

The Jaguar does not have particularly long legs even with external tanks. Therefore, in-flight refuelling is a fundamental part of everyday Jaguar operations, particularly in respect of its role as part of NATO's Rapid Reaction Force. Here, XZ106 'R' takes on fuel while XZ360 'N' waits its turn.

choke points. For the deployment north in a peacetime exercise, the unit would move with all 230 personnel, fly-away packs (FAP) being airlifted by C-130 Hercules transports. The Jaguars themselves would either be in-flight refuelled, or stage through either Sola or Orland. In the event of a real-life situation, the squadron would deploy in small elements as soon as practicable and for this eventuality the FAPs were maintained at all times.

Incorporated within the 230 personnel and equipment was the Reconnaissance Intelligence Centre (RIC). This comprised a number of Air Transportable Reconnaissance Exploitation Laboratories (ATRELs) that were linked together to form film processing and photographic interpretation sections.

The photo-reconnaissance role called for the film magazines to be downloaded from the aircraft and rushed to the RIC immediately on engine shutdown.

Low-level mixed formations are not that common. On this occasion, Jaguar GR.1A XZ113 'FD' was leading an element for the Queen's birthday flypast with a pair of No.20 (Reserve) Squadron Harriers for company.

The introduction of the new all-over grey colour scheme in 1995 led for a while to a dearth of unit markings. Here, XZ363 'FO', is seen in the company of XZ366 'FS' and a pair of Tornado F3s of No.43 Squadron. All appear as 'plain Jane'.

The film was then machine-processed at a speed of 120ft per minute before being displayed and analysed on a light table by an assessing interpreter in consultation with the pilot. However, as there is the likelihood that the pilot could be re-tasked, either immediately on arrival, or even while still airborne, as a backup first of all the pilot would, once in friendly skies, give a 'vis-rep' on a secure frequency to whichever agency he was working for. This comprised details of what he observed visually on the run to the target, together with details of his call sign, heading, height, and so on. This was also recorded in the cockpit on tape, which, together with his flight card, would be handed to the RIC personnel from the cockpit on landing so that interpretation could go ahead even if the pilot was unable to be present.

The RIC itself was completely self-sufficient, with its own generators, water supply and other facilities. ATRELs could be transported either by air, in C-130 Hercules aircraft, or by road, on 4-ton trucks, as required, and could, as such, match the mobility of the squadron.

The Jaguars assigned to Nos II (AC) and 41 (F) Squadrons were drawn from two very distinct batches due to the modifications necessary for operation of the reconnaissance pod and therefore saw very little exchange between units, unlike those that have been assigned to the strike/attack squadrons. The aircraft came from the ranges XZ101-120 and XZ355-367. In time, however, when all three Coltishall squadrons had mirrored roles, these aircraft would become common user.

Although the tactical reconnaissance role became the prime tasking of the two Tornado GR.1A squadrons, No.41 (F) Squadron still retained this role in support of the AMF. The smaller Vinton Vicon 18 Series 601 GP(1) pod, with less of a weight penalty, was introduced post-Operation Granby, when it became apparent that more medium-level reconnaissance would be required. Containing a single F144 camera with an 18in lens (since replaced by a new generation

450mm lens of much higher resolution) and a single Type 900A/B panoramic camera, the superior resolution gave the same stand-off capability as the old 603 pod, but looked at a larger field of view. However, its reliance on wet film technology would mean that this would be no more than an interim solution, and therefore only twelve pods were ordered and these tended to remain in theatre.

The development of the JRRP, or the Vicon 18 series 601 EO GP (1), breathed new life into the Jaguar as a reconnaissance platform and throughout the nineties the jet has fulfilled vital missions policing the former Iraqi No-Fly zone and most of these have been on reconnaissance dedicated sorties. The squadron also took the lead in the JRRP development with the pod entering service alongside the introduction of the Jaguar GR.3A.

JRRP quickly proved its worth over the old wet film Vicon pod. A Type 8040 sensor replaced the old F144 although retaining the same optics whilst a pair of oblique Type 8010 sensors (Electro Optical equilivant of the F95) can be fitted as an option. The Type 900 panoramic camera is in turn replaced by a Vigil infra-red linescan that uses elements of the Tornados TIRRS. The Jaguars unique helmet mounted sight (HMS) has given the pilot a look and shoot capability and this can be coupled to the new pod for target designation. The main advantage of JRRP is the automated nature of the system, which is fully integrated with the Jaguars avionics and navigation system and thus can automatically acquire targets. Therefore when faced with hostile ground fire the pilot has the option to manoeuvre more aggressively whilst still tracking the target. Initially four new pods were procured whilst these were to be augmented by conversion of four of the original pods.

The Achilles heel is still, however, the necessity to return to base for the imagery to be downloaded onto a PC-based system for analysis. Trials have been ongoing to look at a data-link system and these were assessed during one of the SAOEUs annual

XZ103 'P' leads the two 'plain Jane' jets, creating a striking contrast in schemes. '103' itself, however, has worn a multitude of schemes, including Arctic for Exercise Strong Resolve in 1995, the ARTF grey with desert pink upper surfaces as part of Trial Flashman and finally as the No.41 (F) Squadron Jaguar solo display mount for the 2005 season.

North American deployments when Squadron Leader Charlie Cook undertook a trial called 'Speak Easy'. This involved a Jaguar data-linking reconnaissance information via a UAV to an AH-64 Apache helicopter using the Symmetic Industries IDM (Improved Data Modem).

Around thirty Jaguars have been retrofitted with the IDM system that allows the pilot to receive accurate target information in the cockpit during the flight. Integration of JRRP through the Jaguars IDM would give the platform an unrivalled ability for real time reconnaissance. However, although feasible, both time and money are not on the side of Jaguar and whilst JRRP will at some point become fully digital and able to be data-linked, it will be others that benefit from this concept. The lead for this development has now passed to XIII Squadron.

The Jaguar Replacement Reconnaissance Pod (JRRP), or JRP for short, was developed by Vicon to meet the medium altitude requirement. Smaller than the old pod with less of a weight penalty, the pod, in its electro-optical form, has been developed further for use by other RAF platforms. Now dubbed the Joint Reconnaissance Pod, it is an asset still used heavily by the Jaguar force.

Low-level training is a skill that has to be practiced on a regular basis to ensure that the ability in that field does not degrade. Here No.41 (F) Jaguar T.4 XX842 'FX' is seen at low level in Cumbria.

Jaguar 96 XZ360 'FN' of No.41 (F) Squadron closes on to the VC.10 tanker before taking on fuel. Fitted to the port outboard station is an AN/ALQ-101(V)-10 noise/deception jamming pod.

Jaguar GR.3s XZ361 'FT' of No.41 (F) Squadron and XX119 'GD' of No.54 (F) Squadron formate off a tanker on refuelling area 7 on 13 October 1998.

Portrait study of Jaguar GR.3A XZ117 'FB' taken from a Tristar KC.1 on Fuji film using a Nikon F90X and a 80–200mm Nikkor zoom lens.

RAF BRUGGEN

The end of an era was reached on 21 August 2001 when the last permanently based combat squadron – No.31 Squadron – of the Royal Air Force in Germany bade farewell to RAF Bruggen. Six Tornado GR.4 aircraft were waved off by the Burgermeister of Niederuchten, Herr Siegfried Wilms. After almost fifty years, the RAF is withdrawing from Bruggen and, indeed, from stationing in Germany as a UK national formation.

They landed at their new home at RAF Marham at 13.31 hrs (UK time) – precisely planned in honour of their squadron number.

Following the decision in 1996 to withdraw the RAF from Germany and close the last remaining flying bases, the drawdown of RAF Bruggen began in April 1999 when No.17 (Fighter) Squadron was disbanded. No.14 Squadron departed for RAF Lossiemouth in January 2001 and No.IX (Bomber) Squadron relocated to RAF Marham in July 2001. No.37 Squadron, RAF Regiment, moved to RAF Wittering in October 2001. The airfield at Bruggen closed in October 2001 and, thereafter, the intention has been that the base would not be used for fixed wing aircraft, although the Army Air Corps would continue to operate from the facility. The site was taken over by elements of the British Army, with the final handover taking place in March 2002.

The Jaguar operated from the base between April 1975, when the first jets for No.14 Squadron arrived, and October 1985, when

RAF Bruggen began receiving the Jaguar in April 1975, with the re-forming of No.14 Squadron. Initially, the squadron was to receive the last of the 'batch one' aeroplanes. Within a year, however, these were exchanged for batch two jets of a higher modification. XX751 was the unit's first aircraft. In this shot, taken on 6 July 1975, it is seen landing at its home base, but was re-assigned to 226 OCU in the following December.

No.14 Squadron made the transition to the Tornado GR.1. In that ten-year period, four squadrons – 14, 17, 20 and 31 – held the front line strike/attack role for the RAF, a role it inherited from the Phantom FGR.2.

No.14 Squadron

No.14 Squadron was the first of the RAF Germany squadrons to convert to the Jaguar, beginning its training under the auspices of 226 OCU in 1974, in parallel with Squadron Nos 6 and 54, destined for RAF Coltishall. The squadron re-formed with Jaguar on 9 April 1975. The first aircraft, Jaguar T.2 XX836, arrived at Bruggen from Coltishall two days earlier, although the last Phantom FGR.2s did not leave until December.

No.14 Squadron originally formed at Shoreham on 3 February 1915 from a nucleus provided by No.3 Reserve Squadron, and worked up on a variety of types before departing for the Middle East in November. It was tasked with Army co-operation duties in Egypt, Palestine and Arabia, and carried out a series of detachments around the region as hot spots occurred. In November 1917, the squadron received RE8s and concentrated on reconnaissance duties until recalled to the UK in 1919, and disbanded in February of that year. Re-formed in Palestine a year later, the squadron remained in the region throughout the interwar years, flying Bristol Fighters and on various duties including air policing, photo survey and many long-distance 'flag waving' flights around the region. Fairey IIIFs and Gordons replaced these in the early 1930s. By the start of the Second World War, No.14 Squadron was flying Wellesley bombers. With the expected advance of Axis forces through Africa, the squadron began bombing targets in Eritrea in June 1940, before re-equipping with Blenheims and a flight of Gladiators by the end of the year. These were used until the summer of 1942, when Marauders were taken on strength and used in the anti-shipping role. During mid-1944, the squadron moved to Chivenor and flew Wellingtons in the anti-submarine role. This continued until June 1945, when the squadron moved to Banff in Scotland and traded its Wellingtons for the Mosquito.

With an administrative disbandment (for one day), No.14 Squadron reformed at Wahn in Germany with Mosquito bombers, and continued with these until Vampires arrived in 1951, supplemented two years later by Venoms. In 1955, No.14 Squadron became a fighter unit and received Hunters for this role. With another short disbandment in 1962, the squadron re-formed at Wildenrath with Canberras in the strike role until June 1970, when Phantoms arrived. Jaguars replaced these aircraft in the fighter/attack role in 1975 while the squadron was at Bruggen, and remained on strength until 1985 when Tornado GR.1s replaced them. In January 2001 they moved to Lossiemouth.

The squadron's re-equipment with Jaguar ran in parallel with that of No.17, with both squadrons reaching effective unit establishment of fifteen Jaguar GR.1s and two T.2s by the beginning of February 1977. This unusually long transition period by the squadron was created by the need to upgrade their mounts mid-way through the re-equipment process.

The squadron received the last of the 'batch one' aircraft in the serial range XX751–XX768 and it operated these until the end

Although having a nuclear strike task, the Germany-based Jaguars trained hard in the more conventional role of modern warfare. XZ372 'AQ' of No.14 Squadron is captured landing at RAF Lossiemouth on 8 October 1977 during an annual bombing competition.

Smart weapons were not introduced on the Jaguar until post-1991, with the integration of TIALD. They could however be carried, and dropped, with designation being provided by another source. XX746 'AB' of No.14 Squadron is seen here taxiing at RAF Waddington on 10 October 1984 during a Mallet Blow exercise with a single LGB on the centre-line. This was the first live drop of such a weapon by Jaguar, with designation provided by a Buccaneer S.2B equipped with Pavespike.

of 1975, when the first 'batch two' aircraft became available. Its earlier mounts were transferred to 226 OCU at RAF Lossiemouth on a one-for-one basis.

The squadron's relatively short period of use of the Jaguar did not hamper its contribution to the overall RAF front line capability. The Jaguar's restrictions at that time, in particular the limitations of strafing and dive-bombing, did limit the aircraft's effectiveness, although this was not publicly acknowledged. Equally, the radios were poor and improvement only came when replaced by the American Magnavox AN/ARC-164. As far as the RAF Germany aircraft were concerned, further improvements, in the shape of installation of the Mk 104 version of the Adour turbofan, did not begin to come until 1978, while the NAVWASS was only replaced with the Ferranti FIN 1064 in the mid-1980s, almost at the end of the Jaguar's tenure in Germany.

That apart, the squadron, utilising the Jaguar's precision attack capabilities to the full, won the Salmond Trophy in 1975, 1976 and 1977 against competition from longer-established Buccaneer, Harrier and Phantom units. In fact 1977 saw the Jaguars of 14, 17, II (AC) and 31 Squadrons take the first four places. The Tornado GR.1 was always waiting in the wings, and it replaced the Jaguars in November 1985. The squadron did, however, have the distinction of being the last of the Bruggen Jaguar squadrons to re-equip. Unfortunately, the squadron also had the distinction of

incurring the first fatal mishap with the Jaguar Force when XX822, coded 'AA', crashed 15 miles north of Alhorn, with the loss of the pilot. As a mark of respect, prototype XW563, the aircraft that became gate guardian at RAF Bruggen, and subsequently at RAF Coltishall, was repainted to represent the crashed aircraft.

No. 17 Squadron

No. 17 Squadron was the second of the RAF Germany squadrons to make the transition to the Sepecat Jaguar GR.1. It undertook the conversion alongside that of its sister squadron, No. 14, during 1975 and 1976. It too received several 'batch one' aircraft in its early period and these were also later transferred to 226 OCU. The 'batch two' aircraft for the squadron began arriving in August 1975, with the full complement of fifteen single-seat GR.1s and two twin-seat T.2s present by February 1977.

No. 17 was formed at Gosport on 1 February 1915 and, after a period of training, embarked for Egypt in November. On 24 December, it began to make reconnaissance flights over the Turkish lines in Sinai, also flying in support of troops engaged with Turkish army units in the Western Desert. Detachments were also to be found in Arabia until July 1916, when the squadron was sent to Salonika as a mixed unit of twelve BE.2Cs for reconnaissance

No. 17 Squadron was the second RAF Germany squadron to re-equip with Jaguar. The jets initially operated uncoded, but the double letter system was introduced in mid-1976. XZ370 'BN' was the 176th Jaguar built, and was delivered to the unit on 4 November 1976, serving with no other squadron. It was retired in less than ten years and assigned to ground instructional training.

XX827 'BM' of No. 17 Squadron was lost in a crash at Nellis AFB on 12 February 1981. It had been delivered initially to No. 14 Squadron but served briefly with No. 20 Squadron before arriving with No. 17 Squadron.

and a scout component of two DH2s and three Bristol Scouts. At first, it was the only RFC unit in Macedonia, but it was later joined by others. In April 1918 it handed over its fighters to the newly formed No.150 Squadron. For the rest of the war, it was engaged in tactical reconnaissance and artillery spotting on the Bulgarian border. In December 1918, the squadron re-equipped with twelve DH9s and six Camels, sending 'A' Flight to Batum to support the White Russian forces and 'B' and 'C' Flights to Constantinople. No.17 was re-formed at Hawkinge on 1 April 1924, with Snipes forming part of the fighter defence of the UK until the outbreak of the Second World War. Successively equipped with Woodcocks, Siskins, Bulldogs and Gauntlets, the squadron remained in the UK during the Abyssinian crisis but, losing most of its Bulldogs as reinforcements for squadrons moving to the Middle East, had to fly Harts for a period. In June 1939, Hurricanes were received and flew defensive patrols until the German attack on France in May 1940. Fighter sweeps were then flown over Holland. Belgian and French airfields were used to cover the retreat of Allied troops. In June the squadron moved to Brittany as the remnants of BEF and RAF units in France were evacuated, retiring to the Channel Islands two days before returning to the UK. No.17 flew over southern England throughout the Battle of Britain, being moved to northern Scotland in April 1941. In November 1941, the squadron sailed for the Far East where war broke out in December. Diverted to Burma, it arrived in January 1942, as Japanese troops neared Rangoon. Defensive patrols were flown until the Rangoon airfields were overrun and No.17 moved north, eventually being cut off from India while operating from Lashio. The surviving aircraft were flown out and the ground personnel made their way across Burma to the Indian border. By the end of May, the squadron had re-assembled at Calcutta and in June received aircraft again for the defence of the area. Ground attack missions began in February 1943 and continued until August, when the squadron moved to Ceylon. Spitfires began to arrive in March 1944 and were taken back to the Burma front in November to fly escort and ground attack missions. In June 1945 it was withdrawn to prepare for the invasion of Malaya and was taken by carrier to the landing beaches near Penang in early September, soon after the Japanese capitulation. In April 1946, it arrived in Japan to form part of the Commonwealth occupation force, until disbanded on 23 February 1948.

On 11 February 1949, No.691 Squadron, based at Chivenor for anti-aircraft co-operation duties, was re-numbered No.17 Squadron, being officially disbanded on 13 March 1951 and passing its tasks to No.3 CAACU, which was formed five days later. No.17 reformed at Wahn on 1 June 1956 as a Canberra PR.7 photographic reconnaissance squadron in Germany, disbanding on 31 December 1969. On 1 September 1970, No.17 re-formed at Bruggen with Phantom FGR.2s, which were flown until December 1975. Conversion to Jaguar GR.1s began in September. In January 1985 the squadron began to convert to Tornado GR1s, the Jaguar element disbanding on 1 March 1985 when No.17 became fully equipped with Tornado GR.1s.

Although 'official' conversion to Jaguar did not commence until September 1975, the first 'batch two' aircraft for the squadron, XX817 and XX818 (the 100th UK production Jaguar), were delivered direct from Warton on 20 August and 15 August respectively. These ultimately took on the individual codes of 'BB' and 'BC' when the tactical coding system was introduced at Bruggen during 1976. 'BA' was the final 'batch one' aeroplane, XX768, which had been transferred from 14 Squadron along with XX765 and XX766. All three were transferred back to the UK in 1976.

The squadron undertook the first 'Red Flag' deployment in October 1978, which proved very successful, and they returned for a second helping in January 1981. However, conversion to

Transiting through Leuchars on 3 September 1982 was No.17 Squadron twin-seat Jaguar T.2 XX836 'BZ'. The jet had arrived from Bruggen and was returning to Germany the same day. Note the three external tanks.

Above Twin-seat Jaguars saw a lot of interchange between units. XX833 'CZ' of No.20 Squadron, seen here, served at various times with 14, 20 and 41 Squadrons as well as 226 OCU. Ultimately, however, it was to become the TIALD research aircraft with the DRA Experimental Flying Squadron at Boscombe Down, where it was christened 'NightCat'.

No.20 Squadron was the fourth squadron at Bruggen to re-equip with Jaguar and, unlike the other three, transitioned from the Harrier GR.1A. It was also the shortest lived of the squadrons, operating Jaguar for only seven years. XZ378 'CH' was delivered new to the squadron in 1977 but was to be placed in long-term store at Shawbury by October 1990, from where it was sold to a private collector in 2005.

Tornado GR.1 beckoned, and the unit stood down on Jaguar operations on 1 March 1985.

In 2003, No.17 became the first RAF squadron to receive the Eurofighter Typhoon. Based at Warton under the 'Case White' programme, its responsibilities were to include the evaluation of the new aircraft and its integration into full squadron service. On 19 May 2005, the squadron officially re-formed, with the presentation of the squadron standard at RAF Coningsby in Lincolnshire, to become No.17 (Reserve) Squadron, the Typhoon Operational Evaluation Unit.

No.20 Squadron

No.20 Squadron became the fourth of the RAF Bruggen squadrons to receive the Jaguar GR.1, and was the shortest lived. Converting from the Harrier GR.1A at Wildenrath in February 1977, the squadron was to only operate the Jaguar for seven years.

Formed at Netheravon on 1 September 1915 from No.7 Reserve Squadron, the unit deployed to France in January 1916 with FE2Bs in the fighter-reconnaissance role. The squadron devised the 'flying circle', where patrolling pilots flew a continuous orbit in formation while their gunners fire outwards, covering each other. A year later, Sergeant T. Mottershead was posthumously awarded the VC for saving the life of his observer, Lt W.E. Gower, after their stricken aircraft had crash-landed and caught fire. Lt Gower managed to escape the burning wreck and, with assistance, dragged his pilot from the wreckage. However, Sgt Mottershead died four days later from his burns, and he became the only RFC NCO to be awarded the Victoria Cross during the First World War.

In 1917, the Bristol Fighter arrived and, with the squadron constantly refining their tactics, fifty-six German aircraft were accounted for in April 1918 alone. In May 1919, the squadron left the Continent for India, and assumed Army co-operation tasks along the North-West Frontier. The trusty 'Brisfits' were finally replaced in 1932 by Wapitis, and then Audaxes three years later. Lysanders replaced these in late 1941, and these were joined by Hurricane 'tank busters' in mid-1942.

In July 1947, No.20 Squadron was disbanded in India, reforming briefly as a target squadron during 1949–51. The squadron was re-formed at Jever in Germany in July 1952 with Vampire fighter-bombers, these lasting barely a year before Sabres arrived for interceptor duties. These aircraft were then replaced by Hunters. The squadron was disbanded at the end of 1960.

No.20 Squadron reformed in July of the following year at Tengah in Singapore, again with Hunters, but in the ground attack role. The squadron spent six months during 1962 in Thailand as a counter to Communist incursions from Laos, but disbanded again during 1970 following the withdrawal of RAF units from the Far East.

By December 1970, No.20 Squadron had reformed at Wildenrath with Harriers, but these were replaced during 1977 with Jaguars. During 1984, Tornado GR1s arrived, and these remained until, under 'Options for Change', the unit disbanded in May 1992. Later that year, the squadron number plate was assigned to the Harrier OCU at Wittering.

The Jaguar's tenure with the squadron was very short-lived, although if you look back through history, squadrons very rarely retained the same hardware for more than a few years – such was the pace of development in aviation. The squadron began receiving its 'batch three' aircraft direct from Warton to Bruggen in 1977. The first, XZ374, arrived on 5 January, although the squadron did not officially re-form until 1 March.

Although the fourth Bruggen squadron to form it received aircraft codes in the CA–CZ range, fitting in nicely in the alpha-numeric system announced the year previously. Its departure from the Jaguar world was as sudden as its arrival, with the squadron standing down on 24 June 1984 and returning as a ready-made Tornado GR.1 squadron at RAF Laarbruch the following day.

No.31 Squadron

The third RAF Bruggen squadron to make the transition from the Phantom FGR.2, No.31 began receiving aircraft on 19 December 1975, with the arrival from Warton of XX968, although its assigned T.2, XX844, had been operating from Bruggen since the previous August. Over the following month a further eight aircraft were to arrive, with the final three being delivered in February, one of which (XX975) arrived by way of Boscombe Down.

Originally formed at Farnborough on 11 October 1915, the first Flight departed for India with its BE.2Cs and Farmans at the end of November, arriving at Risulpur, India, on 26 December. The two

Unusually, this twin-seat Jaguar T.2, XX844 'DZ' of No.31 Squadron, was to see early retirement in 1990, suggesting that it perhaps suffered a non-cost-effective problem at some point.

During the Cold War period there were many UK and NATO-led exercises that resulted in an abundance of aircraft visiting 'out-of-theatre' stations. Here, Jaguar GR.1 XZ391 'DP' of No.31 Squadron is seen at RAF Coningsby on 25 March 1982, during a UK air defence 'Priory' exercise. Note the construction of Coningsby's hardened aircraft shelters in the background.

remaining Flights had arrived by May 1916, and the squadron spent the remainder of the First World War on co-operation duties with the Indian Army. September 1919 saw the BE.2s finally replaced by Bristol Fighters, and over the next decade these gave sterling service, not only on co-operation tasks, but also during the famous evacuation of Kabul, where they were used to escort Victoria transports. During the 1930s, Army co-operation duties continued, but with Wapitis, until, in April 1939, the squadron changed to the bomber transport role, for which Valentias were employed.

These obsolescent biplanes performed admirably, transporting troops and supplies around the area and bombing rebel villages with great effect. During 1941, the squadron began to concentrate on transport duties with seconded Douglas DC-2s, and these aircraft flew supplies into the beleaguered enclave at Habbaniya in Iraq along with the surviving Valentias. Following its return to India, the squadron re-equipped with the Dakota, and, after the Japanese invasion of Burma, they flew between Calcutta and Rangoon dropping supplies for the XIVth Army.

After the war, the squadron moved to Java, and it was while flying from Kemajoran that one of the Dakotas crashed, and the survivors were hacked to death by Indonesian freedom fighters. Barely a year later, the squadron was disbanded in Java and reformed at Mauripur, India, after the re-numbering of No.77 Squadron. No.31 continued its transport duties until the end of 1947 when it was again disbanded. It was re-formed once again the following July, this time at Hendon following the re-numbering of the Metropolitan Communications Squadron.

A variety of smaller transports were flown on liaison duties around the UK, and these included Ansons, Proctors, Spitfires and even Tiger Moths. In 1955, the unit reverted to its previous identity, and No.31 Squadron moved to Laarbruch in Germany and received Canberra PR.7s – a type it flew until 1971 when they were replaced by Phantom FGR.2s. Operation of the Jaguar GR.1 received during 1976 was nearly as short-lived as it was with its sister squadron, No.20. Conversion to Tornado GR.1 came in 1984 when it stood down from Jaguar operation on 31 October. During the Jaguar's eight-year reign here, the squadron were assigned codes in the DA–DZ range, and joined No.17 Squadron at Nellis AFB for 'Red Flag' in February 1981. Unfortunately, it never had the luxury of growing with the Jaguar as it started receiving appropriate upgrades to allow it to sharpen its claws.

No.II (AC) Squadron was the first dedicated Jaguar reconnaissance squadron. Forming at RAF Laarbruch in 1976, the squadron managed, in the short term, to hang on to its heritage coding system of 'SHINY TWOER JAG' on its twelve aeroplanes. XZ101, pictured here at RAF Leuchars while attending the 1978 tactical fighter meet, is in the in-between stage of adopting a two digit number coding system. The jet retains the individual letter 'S' on the nose wheel door but, akin to its neighbour, has lost the code from the fin.

Currently the squadron forms part of the Marham Tornado Strike Wing alongside No.IX Squadron.

RAF LAARBRUCH

'Eine Feste Burg.' It means 'a strong fortress', and was the motto of RAF Laarbruch since the first RAF fighter flew into the newly built station back in 1954. Boldly displayed on the station's badge, the motto speaks volumes about the role of the base in the time since that first flight, for RAF Laarbruch was one of the key locations from which the Cold War was 'fought' and won.

Located in the town of Weeze in the rural Niederrhein region of Germany, and adjacent to the border with the Netherlands, the station was at the forefront of NATO defences for over four decades. In that time, the station consistently operated some of the most capable and effective aircraft in Europe, including Canberras, Buccaneers, Chinook and Puma helicopters, Harriers, Jaguars and Tornado GR.1s.

The station closed on 30 November 1999, was handed over to the Federal German authorities, and is now the Niederrhein International Airport.

RAF Laarbruch was originally designed to function as a reconnaissance base, operating Meteor and Canberra aircraft.

Visibility from the back seat of the Jaguar T.2 is very good.

As the home, after 1992, of the Harrier and Support Helicopter forces in Germany, Laarbruch came a long way. Although the Cold War is now over, the role of the station remained as vital as ever until the RAF withdrew from Germany. The station supplied aircraft and personnel for Operation Desert Storm, and supported operations over Iraq as part of Operation Provide Comfort (the no-fly zone in northern Iraq) and more recently over Bosnia as part of Operation Decisive Edge (formerly Deny Flight).

Jaguar's involvement at RAF Laarbruch centred solely around No.II (AC) Squadron, which was in situ between February 1976 and January 1989, when the final two aircraft left.

The letter code system lasted a relatively short period before the introduction of a double digit number running between 21 and 34. XZ108 depicted here coded '28' had originally been 'W'.

Above To commemorate the unit's seventy-fifth anniversary XZ104 received special marks, and is captured here on rotation during a sortie from its home base of RAF Laarbruch.

For the RAF, one of the less attractive options of flying in Germany was the height restriction of no lower than 1,000ft. In the UK you can fly down to 250ft almost everywhere and 100ft in specially designated areas.

No.II (AC) Squadron

The first Jaguar to arrive at RAF Laarbruch for No.II (AC) Squadron was XZ101 on 26 February 1976. The remaining eleven single-seaters followed over the next two months. The unit's twin-seat T.2, XX843, was transferred in from 226 OCU in the same period.

No.II (AC) Squadron RFC was formed on 13 May 1912 at Farnborough just one month after the Royal Flying Corps itself was created. The squadron, along with No.3 Squadron, had the distinction of being the first fixed wing flying squadrons to be created in the world (No.1 Squadron flew balloons). Thus the precedent was set for II (AC) Squadron to establish a number of firsts throughout its history.

Using a mixture of BE, Maurice Farman, Breguet and Cody machines, the squadron's first commanding officer, Major C.J. Burke, spent the first two years training the squadron in its reconnaissance role. The squadron has retained this role to the present day.

Deploying to France initially, the squadron was tasked with reconnaissance duties including missions during the battle of Neuve Chapelle, where cameras were used for the first time to record enemy trenches. It was not long, however, before the importance of bombing was realised. One of these bombing missions was carried out on 26 April 1915 by Second Lieutenant Rhodes-Moorhouse. Hitting his objective, a railway junction at Courtrai, with a 100lb bomb, Rhodes-Moorhouse came under heavy fire and was badly wounded. Despite his serious injuries he managed to pilot his plane back to base and insisted on giving a full report before going to hospital. Unfortunately, he died from his wounds the following day. For his gallantry and courage he was awarded a posthumous VC, the first to be gained by the RFC.

The squadron continued primarily in the reconnaissance role in close co-ordination with the Army, and soon gained an impressive reputation. In 1918 the squadron was to record its second VC, this time through Second Lieutenant A.A. McLeod. While on a mission, McLeod's Armstrong Whitworth FK8 was attacked by eight enemy aircraft, but, through skilful manoeuvring, he enabled his observer, Lieutenant A.W. Hammond, to shoot down three of the enemy. During the fight the aircraft's petrol was set alight, forcing McLeod and Hammond – although slightly wounded – to stand

on the lower wing, side-slipping the aircraft to keep the flames away in order to fly the machine and enable Hammond to shoot another enemy aircraft down. The FK8 aircraft inevitably crashed into no-man's-land, badly injuring the observer. However, McLeod unselfishly dragged the observer back to friendly lines where McLeod was wounded further by a bomb. McLeod recovered from his wounds and was awarded the VC for his heroic deeds.

As such, the tone was set for II (AC) Squadron, and its role of armed reconnaissance continues to the present day. Its association with Germany began at the end of the Second World War when, in June 1945, a move was made to Celle, Germany. With the addition of the Spitfire PR XIX in early 1946, a two-flight system evolved, with one flight concerned with high-altitude reconnaissance and the other with low-level tactical reconnaissance. In November

Once clear of the base, the terrain surrounding that part of Germany soon opens out into flat farmland as XZ104 levels out en route to its target.

XZ104 and XZ112, the latter featuring heavily in this portfolio, fly in close formation on the return leg to Laarbruch.

1950 the jet age arrived, and the squadron re-equipped with Meteor FR.9 aircraft, concentrating solely on the low-level tactical reconnaissance role, a capacity in which the squadron continues to operate to this day. During the 1950s the squadron moved to a variety of locations within Germany, and during that time was presented with its standard by Air Chief Marshal Sir Robert Foster. In 1956, the squadron re-equipped with the first reheat capable aircraft, the Supermarine Swift FR.5. This proved a troublesome aircraft but was nevertheless successful in the reconnaissance role. In April 1961 the Hunter era arrived when the squadron re-equipped with the Hunter FR.10 in early 1961. This aircraft was to remain with the squadron for ten years at RAF Gutersloh.

In September 1970, the squadron excelled itself when it won the North European Command 'Big Click' tactical reconnaissance trophy, defeating squadrons from Germany, Norway and Denmark; this was all the more remarkable as many of the targets were maritime, an area in which the squadron had little practice. Later that year the squadron took delivery of the McDonnell Douglas Phantom at Bruggen, the first two-seat aircraft on the squadron since the Lysander days. In March 1971, Hunter operations ceased at Gutersloh, and two months later, II (AC) Squadron moved to Laarbruch, where it was to stay for the next twenty years. To support the squadron, Nos 3 and 4 MFPUs (Mobile Film Processing Units) amalgamated to form the newly named

A shot of the camera ship, XX842 '33', for the sortie on 6 June 1988. The aircraft went on to serve with all the UK-based squadrons and was upgraded to Jaguar T.4 in July 2000, before undertaking Adour 106 upgrade trials at Warton. It will be one of the last Jaguars flying.

RIC (Reconnaissance Intelligence Centre), which formed in Air Transportable Reconnaissance Exploitation Laboratories (ATREL) cabins and was fully mobile. It was also at this time that the squadron markings where revised to two white triangles flanking a white circle containing the 'wake' knot and the aircraft tail letter within a white triangle on the fin (little-known fact – all the tail letters spell the words SHINEY TWO AC!).

In 1976, following a remarkable achievement – no serious incidents occurring during the Phantom period – the squadron converted to the Jaguar to become the longest-serving of all the

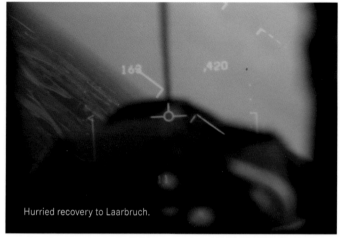

Hurried recovery to Laarbruch.

XZ362 and XZ364 outside Laarbruch's HAS site, configured for the attack role rather than armed reconnaissance.

RAF Jaguar squadrons within RAF Germany. As stated earlier, a full complement of aircraft had been received by the end of April 1976. The squadron was never to succumb to the policy of the double letter codes applied elsewhere in the RAF front line. Initially the Jaguars adopted the single letter codes as described above that spelt 'SHINY TWOER JAG' in order on aircraft XZ101–105, XX843, XZ108–109, XZ106–107, XZ110–112, but, in the summer of 1980, they adopted a two digit number code, portrayed in a similar fashion. This ran from 21 through to 33, although XZ102 was been lost in a crash 10km north of Laarbruch on 14 December 1976, and naturally was not re-coded its place as 'H'. Subsequently, '22' was taken by XZ366, which was from the operational reserve at RAF Abingdon. This system was to remain with the Jaguar until the end of its time with II (AC) Squadron, even with the increase in unit establishment – three additional GR.1 aircraft (XZ361, 362, and 364 – codes 20, 19 and 18 respectively) and a second T.2 (XX845 – code 34). When the Tornado GR.1A was taken on strength the squadron reverted back to the original letter code system.

The squadron saw very little in the way of aircraft change during the Jaguar period, and this has been the same in the era of the dedicated Tornado GR.1A. Apart from the crash of XZ102, mentioned earlier, and the loss of two jets in a mid-air collision in Canada, together with the transfer of one aircraft, XZ107, to No.6 Squadron in 1982, the squadron was to retain the same complement of Jaguars for its entire thirteen-year history, although some re-coding did take place. Not constrained by the reconnaissance fit, it was to operate five different twin-seat Jaguar T.2s, although, from the coding sequence, it retained only two on strength at any one time. The final operational Jaguar sortie by the squadron was undertaken on 16 December 1988, with the final two squadron aircraft departing Laarbruch for pastures new on 27 January 1989, when XZ111 '31' and XX840 '33' were flown to RAF Shawbury and RAF Coltishall respectively.

In 1989, II (AC) Squadron became the first RAF Tornado GR.1A reconnaissance squadron, which represented a change in the direction of tactical reconnaissance, as infra-red linescan video replaced the old photo-reconnaissance print method. The new system had a number of teething problems. However, the unexpected troubles that occurred in the Gulf region in 1991 acted as a catalyst to solve the majority of the GR1.A's problems and, at the eleventh hour, a detachment of six aircraft, consisting of crews from II (AC) and XIII Squadrons, was sent to Dhahran, Saudi Arabia, to prepare for war. During the ensuing conflict, No.2 (Composite) Squadron operated purely at night with a tactical reconnaissance capability that no other Allied squadron could achieve, producing valuable and timely reconnaissance material for the coalition forces.

After the war, the squadron returned to Laarbruch and stayed until December 1991, when it moved to RAF Marham, after an absence of over forty-seven years from England.

CHAPTER 4

BAC/BAE SYSTEMS-PRODUCED JAGUAR AIRCRAFT
Abridged Histories

GLOSSARY OF TERMS USED:

A&AEE	Aeroplane & Armament Experimental Establishment	JMU	Jaguar Maintenance Unit
BDRT	Battle Damage Repair Training	LRMTS	Laser Ranger and Marked Target Seeker
DARA	Defence Aviation Repair Agency	MU	Maintenance Unit
DERA	Defence Evaluation & Research Agency	nwd	Nose wheel door
D/D	Date Delivered	RAE	Royal Aircraft Establishment
DRA	Defence Research Agency	SoTT	School of Technical Training
DTEO	Defence Test and Evaluation Organisation	SAOEU	Strike Attack Operational Evaluation Unit
ETPS	Empire Test Pilots School	TIALD	Target Illumination and Laser Designation
F/F	First Flight	UN	United Nations
FJTS	Fast Jet Test Squadron	wfu	Withdrawn from use
		W/O	Written Off

XW560	S06 rolled out 18/08/69, F/F 12/10/69 (J.L. Dell) and used in handling trials, flutter and structural testing. W/O 11/08/72 in a rear-end ground fire at Boscombe Down and wfu after return to Warton. Used as static test aircraft for gun trials. Centre fuselage to Lossiemouth for instructional duties by 09/73 before relocating to the JMU at Abingdon by 10/77. Finally moving to Coltishall in 06/79 before disposal. Cockpit preserved Boscombe Down.
XW563	S07 rolled out 25/03/70. F/F 12/06/70 (J.L. Dell) and used as trials aircraft with the Elliot digital inertial navigation and weapon aiming system (NAVWASS). On flight 601 undertook F/F with 'Magic' missiles on over-wing pylons. At completion of trials the aircraft was delivered to RAF Bruggen for instructional duties on 26/01/78. Allocated maintenance serial 8563M and, following a period with No.431MU, the airframe was mounted as gate guardian, sporting the spurious serial 'XX822' and coded 'AA' in No.14 Squadron markings as a memorial to the loss of that actual aircraft on 02/07/76 and the first fatality involving the Jaguar aircraft. After the closure of RAF Bruggen the airframe was relocated to RAF Coltishall, Norfolk, where it serves the same purpose.
XW566	B08 F/F 30/08/71 (P. Millett) and differed from S07/S08 in that the airframe was made up predominantly of production parts, enabling it to be tested towards production standard. Testing undertaken at both Warton and Boscombe Down before transfer to the RAE at Farnborough on 3 February 1982 after ten and a half years at Warton and 718 flights. L/F17/06/85 and wfu shortly afterwards and now preserved at Farnborough.
XX108	S1 F/F 01/10/72 (T.M.S. Ferguson), D/D Boscombe Down 27/04/73 for testing by 'A' Squadron. Alternated between A&AEE and BAC and involved in spinning trials between 1977 and 1979, followed by engine development work. Bailed back to the company for the 1979 Paris Salon as G-27-313 where it suffered a nose wheel collapse during a short-field take-off/landing demonstration. By road to the Jaguar Maintenance Unit (JMU) at RAF Abingdon where new nose section was fitted, returning to Warton on 07/08/80. While undergoing overhaul with 19MU at RAF St Athan in 02/94, received 'Children in Need' inscription. Upgraded to GR.1B standard at St Athan mid-1996. Returned to Warton in 2000 to undertake Adour 106 flight trials before making its last flight back to St Athan on 28/05/02. Presented to the Imperial War Museum, it is currently stored at Duxford pending display.

XX109	S2 F/F 16/11/72 (P. Millett), D/D Boscombe Down 01/05/73 for use by 'A' Squadron, A&AEE. To Warton in 03/79 where it undertook motorway landing/take-off trials on an unopened stretch of the M55 near Blackpool over the period 26–27 April 1979. Retained for engine development work, the aircraft was retired in 1986 and was D/D to RAF Coltishall on 21/10/86 with Fl. Lt Mike Rondot as pilot for use as a weapon load training instructional airframe, and given the maintenance serial 8918M. Receiving the code 'US' in 1996, and then repainted in desert pink ARTF colour scheme by May 1998 it was finally retired from use in 2004 and presented to the City of Norwich Museum on 01/09/04.
XX110	S3 F/F 01/03/74 (J.J. Cockburn) and D/D to A&AEE at Boscombe Down early in 1974. Flown to No.60 MU RAF Leconfield on 26/04/76, the aircraft was retro-fitted with the modified nose section containing the laser ranger and delivered to No.6 Squadron the following month. Receiving the individual code of 'EP' it served with the squadron until 24/07/85 when it was dispatched to RAF Shawbury for storage. Allocated the maintenance serial 8955M, it was delivered to No.2 (now No.1) School of Technical Training (2 SoTT) at RAF Cosford, where it resides today.
XX111	S4 F/F 17/04/73 (D. Eagles) and D/D RAF Lossiemouth 30/05/73 for use by No.226 Operational Conversion Unit (226 OCU). Receiving the individual code '01' it served with the unit until 16/11/76 when it was flown to the JMU for fitting of the modified nose section. This was completed early in 1977 and the aircraft was placed into operational store on 06/05/77. Released from store and flown to Warton on 16/10/79 by Eric Bucklow as G-27-314 as part of the Indian Air Force loan deal. Upgraded to 'Jaguar International' configuration and F/F 21/12/79. The jet was delivered to the Indian Air Force as JI 011 on 13/02/80 but was lost on operations on 10/04/82.
XX112	S5 F/F 02/05/73 (T.M.S. Ferguson) and D/D to Boscombe Down for use by 'A' Squadron A&AEE 17/09/73. To JMU store by 09/78, and was re-issued to No.6 Squadron 18/10/79. Sported white diamond marking on tail and upper wing surface in 10/80. The jet was upgraded to GR.1A standard at the JMU in early 1985, returning to No.6 Squadron on 25/01/85 receiving the individual code of 'EA'. Recorded 'EC' by 05/90, the aircraft received the ARTF desert pink scheme for participation in Operation Granby in 08/90. Replaced in theatre it returned to Coltishall and regained its 'EC' code. Dispatched to St Athan for upgrade to Jaguar 96 configuration on 04/03/97, it returned to the squadron as 'EA' on 23/02/98. Re-designated Jaguar GR.3 it received the ARTF grey scheme for overseas operations in 02/03 before once again being dispatched for upgrade to GR.3A configuration. In 10/03 it received No.6 Squadron '60th Anniversary' markings and it still appears on squadron strength today.
XX113	S6 F/F 31/05/73 (P. Ginger) and D/D to Boscombe Down for use by 'A' Squadron A&AEE 18/10/73. Following overhaul at 60MU in 1975 it was D/D to 226 OCU on 22/12/75, taking up the individual code of '09'. Repainted in all-over wrap-around colours at 5 MU RAF Kemble in August 1976, it returned to the unit until lost in a crash on 17/07/81 near Malvern while on a test flight from the JMU at RAF Abingdon.

Delivered on 31 October 1973, XX117 served initially with 226 OCU before being loaned to India. Upon its return to the UK it was subsequently upgraded to GR.1A, Jaguar 96 and finally GR.3A. Although it survived the No.16 (Reserve) Squadron disbandment, it was eventually retired in September 2005.

XX114	S7 F/F 05/07/73 (P. Ginger) and D/D to RAF Lossiemouth on 13/09/73 after being used at Warton on RAF conversion training, becoming individual code '02' with 226 OCU. Repainted in wrap-around camouflage at 5 MU RAF Kemble during April 1976 it was lost on take-off from RAF Lossiemouth while operating with 226 OCU on 19/09/83, with the pilot successfully ejecting. Remains passed to JMU with wings being noted in March 1984. Wreck eventually disposed of to Park Aviation, Faygate, Sussex.
XX115	S8 F/F 16/08/73 (J.J. Cockburn) and D/D to RAF Lossiemouth 13/09/73, becoming code '02' with 226 OCU. This was the first aircraft to be fitted with the RWR on the fin. Passed into operational store with JMU in 27/01/78 until resurrected for use in Indian loan deal, returning to Warton as G-27-315 on 10/07/79. Upgraded to 'Jaguar International' standard it was delivered to India as JI 005 on 11/12/79. Following delivery of IAF new aircraft the jet was flown back to RAF St Athan on 23/07/82 before transferring to No.27 MU at RAF Shawbury for storage. Allocated maintenance serial 8821M, it was issued to No.1 SoTT at RAF Halton in 08/84, although the centre fuselage was noted with the JMU just prior to this. This section was eventually issued to No.2 SoTT at RAF Cosford, where it is believed to be currently.
XX116	S9. Rolled out 22/08/73 and F/F 10/09/73 (T. Ferguson). D/D to RAF Lossiemouth 02/10/73 for use by 226 OCU as individual code '04'. Repainted in wrap-around camouflage at 5 MU RAF Kemble in October 1976, it was passed into the JMU operational store on 22/02/78. Identified as part of the IAF loan deal, it was flown back to Warton as G-27-316 on 02/08/79 for upgrade to 'Jaguar International' standard before being delivered to India as JI 008. It returned to the UK on 19/04/84 direct to Warton for storage. Upgraded to GR.1A standard, the aircraft was re-issued to No.6 Squadron as 'EE' before being transferred to 226 OCU on 09/12/86 to become code '02'. After 226 OCU became No.16 (Reserve) Squadron, the jet received an all-over black colour scheme with a yellow 'Saint' emblem on the tail for the 1993 air-show season. Allocated individual code 'B' it received the new standard all-over grey colour scheme by 05/97, when it was transferred to No.6 Squadron as aircraft 'EO'. The jet became the second Jaguar 97 trials aircraft in January 1999, although retaining its nominal 6 Squadron allocation. Alternated between DERA, the manufacturer, and the front line, until it was retired and wfu at St Athan in March 2005.
XX117	S10 F/F 08/10/73 (D. Eagles) and D/D to RAF Lossiemouth on 31/10/73, where it took up the individual code '05' with 226 OCU. Delivered to 60 MU for nose retro-fit in April 1975, it was then issued to No.6 Squadron on 29/04/76. After a short period at 5 MU RAF Kemble to receive the wrap-around all-over camouflage, the aircraft alternated its time between the front line and trials work at Boscombe Down with the A&AEE. Passed into operational store with the JMU on 25/03/77, it was identified for the Indian loan deal, returned to Warton as G-27-317 on 15/06/79. After upgrade to 'Jaguar International' the aircraft was delivered to India as JI 004 on 14/10/79 returning to the UK (Warton) on 24/02/84, where it was upgraded to GR.1A standard. Re-issued to No.54 Squadron as 'GG', by 11/84 it moved on to 226 OCU by 03/86 as '06'. Transferred into short-term store with 27 MU in 10/90 it was re-assigned to the RAE at Farnborough on 25/01/91, although it retained the marks of its former owner. Upgraded later to Jaguar 96 configuration and used by the SAOEU at Boscombe Down, the jet returned to St Athan for overhaul in early 1998 before re-issue to No.6 Squadron at Coltishall, where it became 'EB'. Transferred to No.16 (R) Squadron as 'A' on 17/12/98 before being re-coded 'PA' on the unit's re-location to RAF Coltishall. Upgraded to GR.3A in 2001, it remained with No.16 Squadron, receiving the unit's special '90th Anniversary' scheme in January 2005. At the demise of the squadron the following March, it was assigned the code 'FS' with No.6 Squadron, which was applied to the nwd. However, service was short-lived. The aircraft was flown to St Athan on 01/07/05, where it was wfu. It was re-assigned as a ground instructional airframe with No.1 SoTT at RAF Cosford, becoming the first of many GR.3A versions to enter the technical training role.
XX118	S11 F/F 24/10/73 (J. Preece) and D/D RAF Lossiemouth for 226 OCU 19/11/73, where it became '06'. Following overhaul at 60 MU the jet was dispatched to 5 MU for repainting in the wrap-around all-over camouflage scheme in March 1976. Following this it was issued to No.6 Squadron at RAF Coltishall on 06/05/76 before dispatch to the JMU for laser nose and RWR retro-fit.

	After returning to No.6 Squadron it passed into short-term operational store with the JMU by 16/01/78. Identified for the Indian loan deal, it was flown to Warton as G-27-318 on 13/02/80 for upgrade to 'Jaguar International' standard.Delivered to India as JI 008 on 11/12/79, it later returned to the UK on 25/05/82, initially to St Athan, and then into store with 27 MU at RAF Shawbury by 12/83. Allocated to instructional use with maintenance serial 8815M, it departed Shawbury on 10/04/84, ostensibly for Abingdon for battle damage repair training. It was noted in 05/84 en-route to the Proof & Experimental Establishment Foulness before returning to the JMU by 11/84. It then was passed to No.1 SoTT at RAF Halton on 23/08/85 but, on closure of that facility, it returned to Abingdon where the fuselage was noted dumped in 02/92.
XX119	S12 F/F 05/11/73 (P. Ginger) and D/D to RAF Lossiemouth 17/12/73 for 226 OCU as individual code '07'. Following overhaul at 60 MU, was re-assigned to No.54 Squadron by 01/09/75. Repainted in wrap-around all-over camouflage at 5 MU Kemble in August 1976, it returned to No.54 Squadron and, when individual code letters were assigned at RAF Coltishall, it became 'GC'. Loaned to the A&AEE during 1982, it had, by 05/86, been re-assigned to 226 OCU again as code '01'. Allocated to ground training shortly afterwards and assigned the maintenance serial 8898M, it never took up this role, and instead remained in service with 226 OCU, being one of the first aircraft to receive the unit's new tartan fin marking in 1994. Became 'A' with No.16 (Reserve) Squadron when the OCU took over this mantle. It was later, following overhaul, assigned the code letter 'E', before receiving the new grey colour scheme in 02/97. Re-assigned to No.54 squadron as 'GD', although loaned to DERA in April 1998, and upgraded to Jaguar 96 configuration. Converted to Jaguar 97 by early 2000, it was re-designated GR.3A two years later, remaining as 'GD' until the demise of No.54 Squadron in March 2005. Allocated the code 'EB' with No.6 Squadron in the subsequent re-shuffle. Flown to St Athan 29/03/06 for store.
XX120	S13 F/F 23/11/73 (E. Bucklow) and D/D to RAF Lossiemouth for use by 226 OCU as code '08'. Following overhaul at 60 MU and subsequent laser nose/RWR retro-fit re-assigned to No.54 Squadron and lost in a crash off Samsoe Island, Denmark, during Exercise Teamwork 76 on 17/09/76.
XX121	S14 F/F 21/12/73 (P. Ginger) and D/D to RAF Lossiemouth for 226 OCU as code '09' on 01/02/74. This was the first aircraft to be fitted with the in-flight refuelling probe and was re-assigned to No.54 Squadron in July 1974. Retro-fitted with laser nose and RWR at 60 MU between 06/08/75 and 11/11/75, the jet was subsequently coded 'GB' with the squadron. Re-assigned to No.6 Squadron as 'EQ' by 07/84, it was passed into long-term store with 27 MU RAF Shawbury by 12/11/84. Taken from store and transferred to Warton in expectation of a follow-on order from the Ecuadorean Air Force. When this failed to materialise, was returned to Shawbury in July 1993. Finally disposed off post-1994 and sold to Park Aviation Supply at Charlwood.
XX122	S15 F/F 11/01/74 (E. Bucklow) and D/D to RAF Lossiemouth for 226 OCU as code '10' 01/02/74. Following overhaul and retro-fit at 60 MU the aircraft was re-assigned to No.54 Squadron on 13/10/75, subsequently taking up the code 'GA' on 26/01/81. It was later lost in an accident on 02/04/82, when the aircraft crashed into the Wash off Heacham. The remains were initially taken to the JMU at RAF Abingdon, before transfer to the AIB at Farnborough on 13/04/82 where they remained until at least 03/86.
XX136	B1 F/F 28/03/73 (J. Cockburn/R. Stock). Flown by Joint Chief of the Air Staff Sir Dennis Smallwood on 23/05/73 and D/D to A&AEE at Boscombe Down 01/06/73, only to be lost in an accident near Winterbourne Gunner on 22/11/74.
XX137	B2 F/F 26/06/73 (P. Ginger/R. Kenward). Evaluated by Kuwaiti pilot L. Duaij on 22/08/73 and by Ecuadorean pilots Col. Pazmino and Col. Mora on 30/08/73. Then used for RAF IP training between 04/09/73 and 26/09/73. D/D Lossiemouth 04/10/73, first aircraft for 226 OCU coded 'A'. Returning to Warton on 05/02/75 as crew ferry for S45 one engine flamed out on approach. Retained for investigation. Unfortunately crashed into Moray Firth on 06/02/76. Wreck recovered and dispatched to JMU on 24/06/76 before later transferring to the AWRE at the PEE Foulness Island where it was still extant in 12/81. Some remains found in the AIB compound at Farnborough in 03/82, with the remainder being sold to Park Aviation Supply, Faygate, Sussex.

XX138	B3 F/F 10/10/73 (J.J. Lee/J. Preece) and D/D 25/10/73 to RAF Lossiemouth for 226 OCU with individual aircraft code 'B'. Overhauled at 60 MU in early 1976, it was dispatched to Warton from Lossiemouth as G-27-319 on 18/12/78, as part of Indian loan deal. Flown to India as JI 001 on 23/07/79 but, at end of loan, sold to Oman as aircraft serial 200 in 01/82. Flown to UK to cure a persistent fuel leak. Arrived JMU 15/09/83, returning to Oman on 13/12/83, where it is still current.
XX139	B4 F/F 05/12/73 (J. Cockburn/S. Boston) and D/D RAF Lossiemouth 03/01/74 for 226 OCU and individual code letter 'C'. Re-assigned to No.6 Squadron by 10/84 as 'ES', it was upgraded to Jaguar T.2A standard in mid-1985 and re-issued to No.226 OCU, taking up its old code. Re-coded 'T' by 03/94 it was loaned to the DTEO in September 1997. Following the T.4 upgrade, it was transferred back to No.16 (Reserve) Squadron as 'T' by January 2000. On 12/04/05 it was flown from RAF Coltishall to St Athan for spares recovery.
XX140	B5 F/F 21/12/73 (D. Eagles/R. Kenward) and D/D RAF Lossiemouth 29/01/74 for 226 OCU, where it took the individual code letter 'D'. Transferred to No.54 Squadron in 07/74 and then back to 226 OCU as 'D' again, until retired to Shawbury on 04/07/85. Allocated the maintenance serial 9008M at No.2 SoTT at RAF Cosford, the jet has subsequently been disposed of, with the hulk passing into the hands of Park Aviation Supply at Faygate, Sussex, by 05/99.
XX141	B6 F/F 25/01/74 (P. Ginger/R. Stock). Evaluated by Belgian AF 20/02/74 and D/D to RAF Lossiemouth 13/03/74 for 226 OCU as individual code 'E'. Converted to Jaguar T.2A configuration by February 1985, when it was issued to No.6 Squadron as 'ET'. It returned to 226 OCU as 'Z' post in 1989, becoming 16 (Reserve) Squadron 'Z' when the unit changed designation by 03/94. Later, by 07/96, it had returned to No.6 Squadron as 'EV' before being retired and becoming a ground maintenance trainer with the 'Aircraft Maintenance Instruction Flight' at RAF Cranwell with maintenance serial 9297M.
XX142	B7 F/F 29/03/74 (J. Preece/A. Love) and D/D to RAF Lossiemouth on 08/05/74 for use by 226 OCU as individual code 'G'. Aircraft later crashed 10 miles north of Lossiemouth on 22/06/79 with the loss of both crew.
XX143	B8 F/F 14/03/74 (J. Preece/E. Bucklow) and D/D to RAF Lossiemouth 18/04/74 for use by 226 OCU as individual code 'F'. Suffered a Cat. 3 bird strike on 29/05/75, causing major damage. Aircraft recovered but did not fly again until 30/03/77. It was later identified for the Indian loan deal and was delivered from Lossiemouth to Warton on 21/12/78 as G-27-321. The jet departed for India as JI 002 on 14/10/79, returning to the UK at RAF Abingdon on 09/09/82. After a period in store, and then overhaul with the JMU, it was re-issued to 226 OCU as 'B' on 17/10/83, before transfer to No.54 Squadron in 08/87, becoming code 'GS' with the unit. Aircraft passed into short-term store with 27 MU at RAF Shawbury in late 1992, before transfer to St Athan to upgrade to Jaguar T.2B standard. However, work was not completed due to limited airframe fatigue life. Returned to service with No.16 (Reserve) Squadron as code 'X' still as a Jaguar T.2A and lost in a crash in the Moray Firth on 18/09/76, shortly after take-off from RAF Lossiemouth. Pilot ejected safely and airframe was recovered by Chinook HC.2 ZA681 'ED' of No.7 Squadron on 25/09/96. Remains sold to Park Aviation Supply at Faygate, Sussex.
XX144	B9 F/F 11/06/74 (J. Preece/D. Wilkinson) and D/D to RAF Lossiemouth 11/07/74 for 226 OCU code 'K'. Suffered an undercarriage collapse on 09/09/74 and was returned to Warton for repairs on 12/01/75. Rebuild completed with F/F 01/10/76. Aircraft was issued to No.54 Squadron on 02/11/76. Transferred to No.6 squadron as 'ET' by 02/81, it was upgraded to T.2A configuration at the JMU during March 1985. Returned to No.6 Squadron strength until transferred to 226 OCU in 08/85, becoming code 'I'. Re-coded 'U' with No.16 (Reserve) Squadron in 05/94, the aircraft was flown to RAF Shawbury for long-term store in early 2000, where it remains today, although its disposal is imminent having been put up for disposal by tender DSAT 3146 on 26/05/05, and destined for Everett Aero, Sproughton.
XX145	B10 F/F 24/05/74 (E. Bucklow/A. Begg) and D/D to RAF Lossiemouth on 14/06/74 for use by 226 OCU as code 'H'. Transferred to the Empire Test Pilots School as a replacement for XX915, it received its 'corporate' red/white/blue colour scheme in mid-1989. Although still on unit charge, the aircraft has now been retired.
XX146	B11 F/F 24/05/74 (J. Cockburn/R. Stock) and D/D to RAF Lossiemouth 10/07/74 for use by 226 OCU as individual code 'J'. Transferred to RAF Coltishall, post-overhaul at 60MU, on 29/10/76, eventually taking up No.6 Squadron markings. Returned to Lossiemouth as 'J' for a short period in 1980/81 but returned to Coltishall on 02/04/81, becoming 6 Squadron 'S'. Transferred to No.41 Squadron but retained same code in late 1983 before passing on to No.54 Squadron as 'GS' in 07/84. Suffered an engine failure on take-off from Coltishall on 30/08/84 but was recovered after pilot jettisoned all external stores. Passed into short-term store with 27 MU between 1987 and 1991, before returning to Coltishall and assignment to No.41 Squadron as 'Y'. Re-assigned to No.16 (Reserve) Squadron as 'J' again in 02/93, before being re-coded 'X' by the following March. Upgraded to Jaguar T.2B configuration and allocated to No.54 Squadron as 'GT', retaining former marks until return from a loan period between 12/95 and 03/96 with the SAOEU, when the new insignia was applied. To St Athan in 04/99 for modification to T.4, returning to No.54 Squadron in 11/00. Finally retired on 07/03/05 when it was flown to St Athan for spares recovery.
XX147	B12 F/F 02/07/74 (E.Bucklow/R.Stock) and D/D to RAF Lossiemouth 20/08/74 for 226 OCU as code 'L'. Re-assigned to No.2 Squadron as 'II' on 30/06/76, it was later transferred to No.17 Squadron as 'BY' and was lost in a crash on 26/03/79 at Sudlohn Borken, West Germany, following a bird strike. Both crew ejected safely.
XX148	B13 F/F 13/08/74 (J.J. Lee/R.T. Taylor) and flown by RSAF pilots on evaluation including C-in-C Lt-Gen. Al-Zuhair. D/D to RAF Lossiemouth 13/09/74 for use by 226 OCU as code M'. Crashed at Whittingham with loss of both crew on 29/07/77.
XX149	B14 F/F 27/08/74 (T. Ferguson/R.T. Taylor) and used in RSAF evaluation. D/D to RAF Lossiemouth 20/09/74 for use by 226 OCU as individual code 'N'. Crashed on 27/04/78 at Cullen, Banff, while en-route Coltishall–Lossiemouth.
XX150	B15 F/F 30/09/74 (A. Love/R. Woollett) and D/D to RAF Lossiemouth 23/10/74 for use by No.6 Squadron, which was forming at the time. To Coltishall 06/11/74 and, following overhaul with 60MU, was re-assigned to No.20 Squadron, followed by No.31 Squadron, where it took the code 'DY'. Transferred on 13/10/82 to No.14 Squadron as 'AZ', it stayed with the unit for a year before once again serving with No.31 Squadron, this time as 'DZ'. Returned to No.14 Squadron as 'AX' by 10/84, remaining with the unit until it converted to Tornado. Flown to 27 MU RAF Shawbury for short-term store in 11/85 and, after overhaul at the JMU, was assigned to 226 OCU as code 'W' by 06/89. Suffered an undercarriage collapse at Lossiemouth on 22/11/90. Following overhaul at St Athan in January 1993 was assigned to No.16 (Reserve) Squadron as 'W' by 03/94. Upgrade to T.4 followed and, after a period of loan with DERA in late 1999 and re-location to RAF Coltishall, was re-coded 'PW'. Transferred to No.41 Squadron as 'FY' in 03/05 following the unit's disbandment. Wfu St Athan by 03/06.
XX719	S16 F/F 31/01/74 (D. Eagles) and D/D to RAF Lossiemouth 04/03/74 for 226 OCU with individual code '11'. Re-assigned to No.54 Squadron 07/74 and eventually coded 'GD' by 02/81 when that station adopted individual code letters. Transferred to No.6 Squadron as 'EB' by 04/85, later becoming 'EQ' and finally 'EE'. Received the ARTF desert pink colour scheme for Operation Granby in 08/90, but was replaced in theatre before war started. Returned to normal scheme and code 'EE' but later sold to Oman following Jaguar 96 upgrade, including TIALD integration. Became serial 226 and was delivered 10/08/98.
XX720	S17 F/F 16/04/74 (T. Ferguson) and D/D to Boscombe Down 08/05/74 for 'A' Squadron A&AEE following preparation for tropical/arctic trials in USA. Flew to CFB Goose Bay with Wing Commander M. Adams on 09/07/74, returning on 13/11/75 to Warton suitably emblazoned with various badges on the fin, including a maple leaf, a Fox's polar bear, and a red 'X' on the ECM pod, having completed nearly 200 flights. Following service acceptance trials flown to JMU and placed in short-term store on 21/02/77. Identified as candidate for Indian loan deal and flown to Warton as G-27-319 on 22/05/79. Following upgrade to 'Jaguar International' standard, delivered to India on 23/07/79 as JI 003 by Chris Yeo via Toulouse, Brindisi, Larnaca, Baghdad, Seeb and Jamnagar, arriving at Ambala after eleven hours airborne. Returned to UK and Warton on 24/02/84 to be brought up to GR.1A standard. Re-issued to No.54 Squadron as 'GQ' on 21/03/85 but, following overhaul at JMU in 02/88 loaned to A&AEE before returning to Coltishall on 03/05/88 for No.6 Squadron and assigned code 'EN'. Received ARTF desert pink colour scheme as

	spare aircraft for Operation Granby. Resumed normal scheme as 'EN' then placed in short-term store at RAF Shawbury between mid-1992 and late 1995. Upgraded at St Athan to GR.1A standard and TIALD-capable. Upon completion assigned to 54 Squadron as 'GB', sporting the new grey colour scheme. Upgraded again as Jaguar 96 before final modification to GR.3A at St Athan in early 2001, returning to 54 Squadron upon completion. Received an Arctic ARTF scheme for Exercise Snow Goose at Bardufoss in 01/05 and transferred to 41 Squadron in 03/05 as 'FL', but was wfu at St Athan by 04/06.
XX721	S18 F/F 06/02/74 (E. Bucklow) and D/D to RAF Lossiemouth 28/02/74 as first production GR.1 for No.54 Squadron, though wore No.11 on the nwd as part of 226 OCU before squadron stood up. Eventually coded 'GE' after squadron moved to RAF Coltishall, but lost in a crash on 12/06/83 near to Hahn while on a NATO exchange visit to the 313th TFS.
XX722	S19 F/F 28/02/74 (J. Preece) and D/D to RAF Lossiemouth 20/03/74 for No.54 Squadron, although carried code '13' of 226 OCU until squadron officially formed. Upon re-location to RAF Coltishall took up the code 'GF' in 02/81 but re-assigned to No.6 Squadron by 05/84, becoming 'EF' in the process. Placed in store at RAF Shawbury on 22/01/85 but transferred to Warton for possible resale to Ecuador. When that fell through the aircraft was returned to Shawbury in 07/93 until transfer to DARA at St Athan for battle damage repair training on 25/06/97. Still current in 03/02 then transferred to the Aircraft Recovery and Transportation Flight, where the nose section currently resides. The remainder was scrapped in 01/06.
XX723	S20 F/F 19/03/74 (E.Bucklow) and D/D RAF Lossiemouth 08/04/74 for No.54 Squadron although initially received code '14' as part of 226 OCU. The move to Coltishall saw code 'GG' assigned before transfer to No.6 Squadron in late 1984, when it took the code 'EQ'. Transferred back to 226 OCU as '07' in 03/86, the aircraft spent periods on loan with the Coltishall squadrons. Re-coded '05' in March 1988 and finally re-assigned to 54 Squadron as 'GQ' at the beginning of 1992. The new grey colour scheme was applied in July 1996 along with upgrade to GR.1B, followed by Jaguar 97 in late 1999. Loaned to DERA and re-designated GR.3A in 11/99, the jet received at least one application of ARTF grey for overseas deployment, and remained with 54 Squadron until its demise, when it was transferred to 41 Squadron as 'FF', with whom it is still current.
XX724	S21 F/F 26/04/74 (D. Eagles) and undertook AAR trials with A&AEE. D/D to RAF Lossiemouth 29/05/74 for No.54 Squadron, although carried the code '15' during the 226 OCU work-up period. When the Coltishall squadrons adopted code letters the aircraft became 'GA', until it passed into long-term store at RAF Shawbury on 27/02/89. Despatched to St Athan on 13/04/99 for overhaul it was returned to 54 Squadron on 26/04/01, only to return to St Athan for GR.3A upgrade on 17/03/03, after which it adopted the code 'GC'. Transferred to No.6 Squadron in 03/05, becoming 'EC' in the process.
XX725	S22 F/F 08/05/74 (E. Bucklow) and D/D RAF Lossiemouth 30/05/74 for No.54 Squadron, temporarily adopting the code '16' for the 226 OCU work-up period. To JMU in 01/79 and identified for Indian Air Force loan, being ferried to Warton as G-27-325 on 20/09/79. Following upgrade to 'Jaguar International' configuration, was flown to India on 13/02/80 as JI 010. Returned to the UK 19/04/84 and into short-term store at Warton. Delivered back to Coltishall on 12/08/85 as a GR.1A, becoming 'EL' of No.6 Squadron. Repainted in the ARTF desert pink colour scheme and one of twelve aircraft to receive over-wing missile rails and uprated engines. It deployed to Thumrait and later Muharraq on 23/10/90. Coded 'T' in theatre and named 'Johnny Fartpants' upon its return to the UK on 13/03/91, it carried forty-seven mission symbols. Re-assigned to No.54 Squadron as 'GU', it retained its ARTF scheme for a period as part of Operation Warden but, on re-painting in 10/92 was inadvertently serialled XX729 on the portside, although this was rectified by 03/11/92. Selected to receive 'stage three' modifications, including fitting of Sky Guardian RWR and wiring for operation of TIALD. It participated in Operation Deliberate Force in the new grey (baby blue) ARTF scheme. In 09/95 was noted wearing seven mission symbols comprising a blue lightning symbol beneath the cockpit on the port side. Normal scheme re-applied in 11/95, the designation having been un-officially altered to GR.1A(T), then GR.1B. Transferred to the SAOEU in 10/96, it returned to the squadron two years later, once again as 'GU'. Upgraded to GR.3 at St Athan during 1999, it alternated between 54 Squadron and the SAOEU for the next few years. Still as 'GU' received the Arctic ARTF finish in 01/05 for participation in Exercise Snow Goose at Bardufoss. Upon its return, it was re-assigned to 41 Squadron.

Caught at medium level, XX720 was the one early Jaguar GR.1 not assigned to No.54 (F) Squadron at its formation, serving instead with the A&AEE. Serving in India for five years it was upgraded upon its return to GR.1A, then subsequently to GR.1A(T), Jaguar 96, GR.3 and, finally, GR.3A.

XX726	S23 F/F 07/05/74 (P. Ginger) and D/D to RAF Lossiemouth for No.6 Squadron. This was the first GR.1 to come off the production line already fitted with the re-designed nose section supporting the laser rangefinder. Ironically, the nose was damaged by a fork-lift truck, delaying its redeployment from Lossiemouth to Coltishall until 12/11/74. Later assigned code 'EB' the aircraft was flown to 27 MU RAF Shawbury during 1985, and then assigned to ground instructional duties at No.1 SoTT at RAF Halton with maintenance serial 8947M. Upon closure of that facility it was transferred to RAF Cosford, where it still resides.
XX727	S24 F/F 14/05/74 (J.J. Lee) and D/D to RAF Lossiemouth 16/07/74 for No.6 Squadron. Receiving the code '21' during its period of work-up with 226 OCU, it departed for Coltishall on 06/11/74. Transferred to No.54 Squadron in 11/75, eventually adopting the code 'GJ' in 01/81. Returned to 6 Squadron as 'ER' in 05/84, only to be flown to RAF Shawbury on 26/07/84. Assigned to ground instructional duties at No.2 SoTT RAF Cosford as 8951M in 1988, where it still resides today.
XX728	S25 F/F 29/05/74 (J. Cockburn) and D/D to RAF Lossiemouth 27/06/74 for 226 OCU, adopting code '18'. During this period it undertook trials on the painting of the aircraft undersides to create an all-over wrap-around camouflage. Re-assigned to No.6 Squadron on 28/10/75, it was later identified as a candidate for loan to India. Flown to Warton as G-27-324 on 10/12/78 and, following upgrade to 'Jaguar International' standard, was delivered to India on 29/04/80 as JI 009. It returned to the UK (St Athan) on 23/07/82, before transferring to JMU on 08/03/83. Re-delivered to No.6 Squadron 11/07/83 as 'EH', it was later upgraded to GR.1A but was lost in a mid-air collision with XX731 on 07/10/85 in the Hartside Pass, Cumbria. Remains were later noted in the Farnborough AIB compound during 03/86.
XX729	S26 F/F 03/06/74 (J. Cockburn) and D/D to RAF Lossiemouth 08/07/74 for 226 OCU as code '19'. Re-assigned to No.6 Squadron on 01/09/75 following overhaul at 60 MU. It received the all-over wrap-around camouflage by 03/76. Identified as a candidate for loan to India it was flown to Warton as G-27-326 on 14/03/79 and, following upgrade to 'Jaguar International' standard, was delivered to India on 19/04/80 as JI 012. Returned to the UK (St Athan) on 25/05/82, before transfer to the JMU on 15/03/83. Re-assigned to 54 Squadron as 'GE' on 25/07/83 and transferred to 6 Squadron as 'EJ' by 06/84. Upgraded to GR.1A in 1987 and re-issued to 226 OCU, eventually becoming code '07'. It was back with 54 Squadron as 'GC' on 31/10/88, moving on to 6 Squadron again as 'EL' following repainting in the new permanent grey colour scheme on 15/03/95. Conversion to GR.1B at St Athan in late 1995 was followed by a number of periods of loan to the SAOEU. Modified to Jaguar 96 configuration at St Athan between 24/09/98 and 25/03/99 and then GR.3A in 2002, remaining on 6 Squadron strength.

Fitted with ARTF painted external tanks, XX738 was serving with No.54 (F) Squadron when captured in this shot during March 1984. Another aircraft to have been part of the Indian Air Force loan, its airframe hours have been husbanded with a three-year period in store at Shawbury. Modified to GR.1B(T), Jaguar 96 and Jaguar GR.3A, it will probably see service until the type is retired from the inventory.

XX730	S27 F/F 13/06/74 (E. Bucklow) and D/D to RAF Lossiemouth 11/07/74 for 226 OCU as code '20'. To No.6 Squadron, leaving Lossiemouth for Coltishall on 06/11/74. Loaned to 54 Squadron for 'Red Flag' deployment in 1980. Was eventually to take up the code 'EC' by 02/81. Flown to RAF Shawbury for storage in 1985 and assigned to ground instructional training in 1988. Allocated maintenance serial 8952M with No.2 SoTT at RAF Cosford, where it still resides.
XX731	S28 F/F 03/07/74 (J.J.Lee) and D/D to RAF Coltishall 23/08/87 for No.54 Squadron. Coded 'GK' in 02/81 before transfer to No.6 Squadron by 04/84. Coded initially 'EK' then, following GR.1A upgrade, 'ED'. The jet was lost in a mid-air collision with XX728 over Hartside Pass, Cumbria, on 07/10/85. Wreck later noted with AIB at Farnborough in 03/86.
XX732	S29 F/F 08/07/74 (E. Bucklow) and D/D RAF Lossiemouth 19/07/74 for No.54 Squadron. Received shark's mouth markings when attending bi-anual 'Bulls Eye' competition at Husum air base, West Germany, in 10/79, and was eventually coded 'GL' in 02/81. Transferred to No.6 Squadron as 'ED' by 10/83 then, following upgrade to GR.1A and overhaul at the JMU between 30/06/85 and 25/09/85, was re-assigned to 226 OCU as '03' on 08/11/85. The aircraft crashed on Stocks Hill in the Craik Forest, 11 miles south-west of Hawick, on 27/11/86, killing the USAF exchange pilot.
XX733	S30 F/F 17/07/74 (J.J.Lee) and D/D to RAF Lossiemouth 21/08/74 for No.6 Squadron. Sported a white circle on tail and upper wing surfaces in 10/80, and was assigned the code 'ED' in 02/81. Delivered to Warton for FIN1064 installation in 09/83 followed by a period of loan with the A&AEE. Re-assigned to 54 Squadron as 'GL' then back to No.6 Squadron again as 'EF'. To JMU in 05/90 for upgrade, including over-wing missile rails and Sky Guardian RWR, the jet was repainted in the ARTF desert pink colour scheme for participation in Operation Granby, departing for the Gulf on 23/10/90. While in theatre, received 'Fighter Pilot' nose art and the code 'R' on nwd. Returned to the UK on 13/03/91 sporting thirty-nine mission symbols. Returned to No.6 Squadron as 'ER' by 06/91 but later had the ARTF grey scheme applied for participation in Operations Grapple and Warden. New permanent grey scheme applied in 06/95, and aircraft re-designated GR.1B. Crashed on take-off from Coltishall on 23/01/96, with the loss of the pilot. Remains stored on base until 10/00, until removed for scrap to Park Aviation Supply, Faygate, Sussex.
XX734	S31 F/F 05/08/74 (E. Bucklow) and D/D RAF Lossiemouth 22/08/74 for No.6 Squadron. To Coltishall 06/11/74 and, following repainting in the all-over wrap-around camouflage at 5 MU Kemble in 11/76, was identified as a candidate for loan to India. Flown to Warton as G-27-328 on 02/05/79. Following upgrade to 'Jaguar International' configuration, was delivered to India on 14/08/80 as JI 014. It returned to the UK (St Athan) on 11/02/82 before transfer to store at RAF Shawbury. Allocated to ground instructional duties as 8816M it departed Shawbury on 10/04/84 and, by way of Farnborough and Abingdon, it arrived at Coltishall for battle damage repair training in 11/84. Later disposed of to Park Aviation, Charlwood.
XX735	S32 F/F 15/08/74 (P. Ginger) and D/D RAF Lossiemouth 13/09/74 for No.6 Squadron. To Coltishall 06/11/74, the aircraft was lost in a crash near Eggebek, West Germany, during Exercise Teamwork 76.
XX736	S33 F/F 27/08/74 (J. Cockburn) and D/D RAF Lossiemouth 30/09/74 for 226 OCU code '11'. To No.6 Squadron 22/12/75 following overhaul at 60 MU and later to JMU. Identified as a candidate for loan to India. Flown to Warton as G-27-327 on 14/11/79 and, following upgrade to 'Jaguar International' standard, delivered to India on 13/02/80 as JI 013. Returned to the UK (Warton) on 24/02/84 and placed in store against potential overseas sales. Transferred to RAF Shawbury, where it was to reside until assigned to ground instructional duties. Allocated maintenance serial 9110M for BDR at RAF Coltishall, where it was noted in 02/92. Nose and tail sections, along with an unidentified centre fuselage section from St Athan dispatched to BAE SYSTEMS at Brough for fatigue testing in late 1996.
XX737	S34 F/F 27/08/74 (E. Bucklow) and D/D to RAF Lossiemouth 27/09/74 for 226 OCU code '09'. Re-assigned to No.54 Squadron following overhaul at 60MU on 22/12/75, but later identified as candidate for loan to India. Flown to Warton as G-27-330 on 30/05/79 and, following upgrade to 'Jaguar International' standard, was delivered to India on 14/08/80 as JI 015. Returned to the UK (St Athan) on 25/05/82 for short-term store. To JMU for overhaul in 03/83, before being re-issued to No.6 Squadron on 25/10/83 as 'EN'. Transferred to 54 Squadron following upgrade to GR.1A, becoming code 'GG'. Was again in short-term store, at RAF Shawbury, between 17/05/89 and 06/11/94, when it returned to No.6 Squadron strength as 'EE'. Upgraded to Jaguar 96 configuration at St Athan in mid-1997 and later to GR.3A in mid-2001. Undertook operational duties abroad during 02/03, when the ARTF grey finish was applied. Wfu St Athan by 03/06.
XX738	S35 F/F 09/09/74 (E. Bucklow) and D/D RAF Lossiemouth 27/09/74 for No.6 Squadron. Departed to RAF Coltishall 06/11/74 and, following overhaul with 60 MU, was identified as a candidate for loan to India. Flown to Warton from Abingdon as G-27-329 14/03/79 and, following upgrade to 'Jaguar International' standard, was delivered to India on 13/02/80 as JI 016. Returned to the UK (Abingdon) on 19/04/84 and, following upgrade to GR.1A, was re-issued to No.54 Squadron as 'GJ' on 27/08/84. Incurred a serious fuel transfer problem on take-off from RAF Chivenor on 11/08/84, forcing the pilot to jettison all external stores into the river Taw before making an over-weight landing. Dispatched to JMU and later to short-term store at RAF Shawbury by 11/90, where it remained until at least 12/93. Received 'stage three' modifications and was re-issued to No.6 Squadron on 12/12/94, but transferred to No.54 Squadron by 02/95 as 'GG'. Received new grey colour scheme during overhaul at St Athan in early 1996, and was re-designated GR.1B (T). Loaned to SAOEU between 24/09/96 and 17/03/97 and upgraded to Jaguar 96 standard by 11/98. Transferred to No.6 Squadron as 'ED' following overhaul in 10/05.
XX739	S36 F/F17/09/74 (E. Bucklow) and D/D to RAF Lossiemouth 23/10/74 for 226 OCU code '12'. Transferred to No.6 Squadron 31/07/75 and repainted into wrap-around all-over camouflage scheme at 5 MU in 08/77. Was carrying white square on tail and upper wing surfaces in 10/80 and coded 'EE' in 02/81. Assigned to the Gibraltar Detachment (Gib Det) as 'I' and then to store at RAF Shawbury in 10/85. Assigned to ground instructional duties in 12/86 at No.1 SoTT RAF Halton with maintenance serial 8902M. Later transferred to RAF Cosford, where it still resides.
XX740	S37 F/F 25/09/74 (A.M. Love) and D/D to RAF Lossiemouth 23/10/74 for No.6 Squadron. To Coltishall 06/11/74 and, following overhaul with 60 MU and transfer to JMU, identified as a candidate for loan to India. Flown to Warton as G-27-331 on 17/03/80 following upgrade to 'Jaguar International' standard. Suffered a nose wheel collapse on landing on 23/04/80. Later delivered to India on 14/08/80 as JI 017. Returned to UK (Warton) 19/04/84 for future export orders, and was sold to Oman as 225 (departing UK on 04/11/86), where it is still current.
XX741	S38 F/F 04/10/74 (J. Preece) and D/D RAF Lossiemouth 18/11/74 for 226 OCU, code '13'. Following overhaul at 60 MU in 11/75, re-issued to No.54 Squadron, eventually becoming 'GL' in 02/81. Transferred to No.6 Squadron and upgraded to GR.1A with code 'EJ'. Received desert pink ARTF scheme in 08/90 and sent to Gulf in interim before 'stage three' upgraded aircraft arrived in 10/90. Returned to UK before conflict, regaining original scheme and code. Transferred to 226 OCU as '04' by 09/93 and sent to RAF

	Shawbury for long-term store by 08/94. Still current in 09/05 although had been put up for disposal by tender under DSAT 3146 on 26/05/05. Departed Shawbury by road for D. Everett Aero, Sproughton, on 18/11/05.
XX742	S39 F/F 21/10/74 (E. Bucklow) and D/D to Boscombe Down 15/11/74 for engine stall trials behind a Victor K.2. Later to RAF Lossiemouth on 09/12/74 for 226 OCU code '14'. Following overhaul at 60 MU between 30/10/75 and 10/12/75, was re-issued to No.6 Squadron on 05/01/76. Received white square markings on tail and upper wing surfaces in 10/80 and was coded 'EF' in 02/81. Aircraft crashed into North Sea, 40 miles off Bacton, Norfolk, on 19/04/83, with the pilot ejecting safely.
XX743	S40 F/F 30/10/74 (E. Bucklow) and D/D to RAF Coltishall 26/11/74 for No.6 Squadron. Coded 'EG' in 02/81, passed into store at RAF Shawbury on 05/02/85, and assigned to ground instructional duties at RAF Halton as 8949M, where it was noted in 03/88. Re-assigned to No.2 SoTT at RAF Cosford on 29/09/94 upon the closure of Halton, and is still in use.
XX744	S41 F/F 07/11/74 (E. Bucklow) and D/D Boscombe Down 05/12/74 for use by A&AEE. Returned to Warton on 18/06/75 and re-issued to No.17 Squadron by 07/76, receiving the temporary code 'S'. Following overhaul at the JMU, transferred to 14 Squadron in 05/78 as 'BU', before changing to 'BG' by 09/78. To No.6 Squadron becoming 'EH' in 02/81 but back in Germany with 31 Squadron as 'DG' by 06/81. Moved to 17 Squadron as 'BA' in 09/83 and back to 31 Squadron as 'DJ' in 01/84. Flown to RAF Shawbury for storage on 07/02/85 but transferred to Warton by 07/93 as a possible re-sale contender to Ecuador, but this never materialised. Returned to store at RAF Shawbury by 08/94, then to ground instructional duties at RAF Coltishall in 05/98. Sold to D. Everett Aero, Sproughton, by 10/02.
XX745	S42 F/F 05/11/74 (E. Bucklow) and D/D to RAF Lossiemouth 16/12/74 for 226 OCU, code '15'. Following overhaul at 60 MU and then repainting in the wrap-around all-over camouflage scheme at 5 MU in 10/76, the jet was re-assigned to No.20 Squadron as code 'CU'. Transferred to 6 Squadron on 09/03/79 and coded 'EJ' in 02/81. At JMU in early 1984 and, upgraded to GR.1A, was re-issued to 54 Squadron as 'GN' in 05/84. Returned to 226 OCU in 12/86, taking up the code '03', before returning to 6 Squadron on 05/08/88 as 'EB'. Once again to 226 OCU on 07/03/89, this time as '04', retaining that code when unit became 16 (Reserve) Squadron. Returned to 6 Squadron in 08/93 as 'EG' before receiving the new grey colour scheme at St Athan. Once again assigned to 16 (Reserve) Squadron in 11/96 as a GR.1A, before transfer to 54 Squadron as 'GV' by 05/99. Involved in a collision with XX832 in 07/00, resulting in damage to the forward fuselage section. By road from RAF Leuchars to St Athan on 25/11/00 and then to store at RAF Shawbury, where it remains today.
XX746	S43 F/F 04/12/74 (E. Bucklow) and D/D to RAF Lossiemouth 20/12/74 for 226 OCU as code '16'. Repainted in all-over wrap-around camouflage scheme at 5 MU in 02/77 and then placed in short-term store with JMU at Abingdon. Issued to No.31 Squadron in late 1977, becoming code 'DE', but transferred to 6 Squadron on 02/04/79, becoming 'EK' in 02/81. To No.17 Squadron 19/08/82 as 'BD' and then on to 14 Squadron by 06/84 as 'AB'. Returned to RAF Lossiemouth on 04/11/85 to once again join 226 OCU, this time as code '09'. This was short-lived, as it was placed in store at RAF Shawbury shortly afterwards. Assigned to ground instructional duties and allocated maintenance serial 8895M it was delivered to No.1 SoTT at RAF Halton by 08/86. Upon closure of this facility it relocated to RAF Cosford, marked as code 'S', where it still resides.
XX747	S44 F/F 04/12/74 (E. Bucklow) and D/D RAF Lossiemouth for 226 OCU code '17'. Repainted into all-over wrap-around camouflage at 5MU in 04/76, it was re-issued to No.54 Squadron by 02/80 for that unit to take the aircraft to 'Red Flag'. Transferred to 17 Squadron 18/01/83, becoming 'BA'. By 09/83 it had moved on to 31 Squadron as 'DG' and finally 20 Squadron as 'CH' two months later. It moved to 6 Squadron as 'EK' by 08/84, forming part of 'Gib Det' as 'B', before being retired to RAF Shawbury by 10/85. Allocated to ground instructional duties with No.1 SoTT RAF Halton, and assigned maintenance serial 8903M. Received ARTF desert pink scheme with spurious 'Sadman' nose art (a la XZ364) and, upon closure of that facility, was transferred to the Aircraft Maintenance Instruction Flight at RAF Cranwell for use by the Airframe Technology Flight where it, or at least part of it, is still current.

With signs of a temporary camouflage finish having recently been removed, XX748, photographed on 7 February 1996, had recently returned from Boscombe Down, where it had become one of the first three Jaguars to be upgraded to carry TIALD.

XX748	S45 F/F 24/12/74 (E. Bucklow) and D/D to RAF Lossiemouth 05/02/75 for 226 OCU as code '20'. Placed in short-term store with JMU by 10/77. It had returned to the unit again by 08/79. Re-issued to 14 Squadron as 'AA' on 15/08/83 but transferred to Coltishall in 10/85 for 54 Squadron, where it took up the code 'GK' then, in 02/87, 'GD'. At RAF Shawbury for short-term store by 02/89, but to JMU for Gulf War upgrade in 05/90, and out-shopped in desert pink ARTF on 02/10/90. The aircraft departed for Thumrait on 02/11/90. Returned 12/03/91 coded 'U' on nwd and sporting thirty-six mission symbols. Back in normal camouflage and as 'GK' by 06/91, it was dispatched to Boscombe Down as one of three aircraft to receive the 'stage three' upgrade allowing the use of TIALD. Initially designated GR.1B then, following attention at St Athan in 07/00, GR.3, and, finally, GR.3A. Retained by squadron as 'GK' until disbandment, then passed to 6 Squadron as 'EG' 03/05.
XX749	S46 F/F 14/01/75 (E. Bucklow) and D/D RAF Lossiemouth 14/02/75 for 226 OCU as code '21'. Suffered a nose wheel collapse while in hangar on 18/04/75 and did not fly again until 10/06/76. To 5 MU for repainting in wrap-around all-over camouflage on 23/06/76, and then to 60 MU for overhaul on 20/07/76. The aircraft crashed on return to the unit on 10/12/79 after colliding with XX755 near Lumsden, West Aberdeenshire, with the loss of the pilot.
XX750	S47 F/F 16/01/75 (P. Millett) and D/D to RAF Lossiemouth on 17/02/75 for 226 OCU code '22'. Repainted in the all-over wrap-around camouflage at 5 MU in 04/76, followed by overhaul at the JMU. Returned to unit but transferred to 14 Squadron as 'AL' on 05/08/83, only to crash in the Nellis Range area during 'Red Flag' on 07/02/84, with the loss of the 6 Squadron pilot.
XX751	S48 F/F 27/01/75 (E. Bucklow) and D/D to RAF Coltishall 14/04/75 for onward transfer two days later to 14 Squadron, where it was coded 'X'. Transferred to 226 OCU on 10/12/75, becoming code '10', and was repainted into the wrap-around all-over camouflage at 5 MU in 04/76. Placed in store at RAF Abingdon and relegated to ground instructional duties by 03/88, when it was assigned maintenance serial 8937M, with No.2 SoTT at RAF Cosford, where it resides today.
XX752	S49 F/F 07/02/75 (P. Ginger) and D/D to RAF Coltishall 04/03/75 for use by 54 Squadron. Following overhaul at 60 MU it was transferred to 226 OCU as code '06' only to be sent to 5 MU for repainting into the all-over wrap-around camouflage scheme. Placed into short-term store with JMU in 03/80 and later upgraded to GR.1A before issue back to 54 Squadron as 'GF' in 05/84. Again placed into store, this time at RAF Shawbury by 12/88. At RAF Shawbury until 29/10/90, when it was sent back to the JMU still marked as 54/GF. Re-issued to No.6 Squadron as 'EQ' by 06/91. Upgraded to GR.3A while at St Athan between 06/09/99 and 22/02/00 and issued to 16 (Reserve) Squadron as 'D' on 01/03/00 and, subsequently, 'PD'. To 41 Squadron as 'FC' by 12/01, and painted in ARTF Arctic colour scheme in 11/03 for Exercise Snow Goose at Bardufoss. Returned to normal grey on 08/12/03 and re-assigned to 6 Squadron as 'EK' in 03/05.

XX753	S50 F/F 24/02/75 (E. Bucklow) and D/D to RAF Coltishall 27/03/75 for use by 6 Squadron. Following overhaul by 60 MU, transferred to 226 OCU on 02/07/76, taking up the code '05'. Repainted at 5 MU in the all-over wrap-around camouflage scheme during 08/77 and loaned to 54 Squadron for 'Red Flag' in 02/80. To store at RAF Shawbury by 11/90. Cockpit section allocated to RAF Exhibition Flight at RAF Abingdon, with maintenance serial 9087M.
XX754	S51 F/F 12/03/75 (J. Cockburn) and D/D to RAF Lossiemouth on 22/04/75 for 226 OCU code '23'. Repainted in all-over wrap-around camouflage at 5 MU in 06/76 and later loaned to No.54 Squadron for 'Red Flag' 02/80. Re-assigned to 14 Squadron on 21/09/84 as 'AL' then back to 226 OCU in 03/85. Upgraded to GR.1A at JMU in 01/87 and transferred to 54 Squadron as 'GR', and then to 6 Squadron by 06/90 as 'EQ'. To JMU in 09/90 for Gulf War upgrades, emerging in desert pink ARTF finish. Delivered to unit at Thumrait on 02/11/90 but crashed prior to hostilities on 13/11/90 in Qatar 100 miles south of Bahrain with the loss of the pilot.
XX755	S52 F/F 12/03/75 (E. Bucklow) and D/D to RAF Coltishall 14/04/75 prior to delivery two days later to RAF Bruggen for use by 14 Squadron. Initially coded 'A', it was only on squadron strength until 07/10/75, when it was transferred to 226 OCU as '08'. Repainted at 5 MU in the all-over wrap-around camouflage during 04/76 it crashed on 10/12/79 near to Lumsden, West Aberdeenshire, after colliding with XX749.
XX756	S53 F/F 21/03/75 (E. Bucklow) and D/D to RAF Bruggen 23/04/75 for 14 Squadron as code 'B'. First Jaguar delivered directly to Germany. Re-assigned to 226 OCU on 08/10/75 as code '07' and was repainted in all-over wrap-around camouflage at 5 MU in 11/76. Transferred to 20 Squadron as 'CB' in 03/84 then to 14 Squadron as 'AB' in 07/84, returning to RAF Coltishall in 10/85. Assigned the maintenance serial 8899M and allocated to ground instructional duties at No.2 SoTT RAF Cosford by 08/86, where it resides today, with the code 'W'.
XX757	S54 F/F 03/04/75 (A. Love) and D/D to RAF Bruggen 06/05/75 for 14 Squadron, code 'E'. Transferred to 226 OCU on 17/10/75, taking the code '12', and was repainted in the all-over wrap-around camouflage at 5 MU in 03/76. Re-assigned to 20 Squadron as 'CU' in early 1980 and placed into store at RAF Shawbury on 04/07/84 where, by 03/88, it had been assigned to the ground instructional role. Allocated the maintenance serial 8948M with No.1 SoTT at RAF Halton, it subsequently moved to RAF Cosford with the closure of that station. It is still current today.
XX758	S55 F/F 11/04/75 (E. Bucklow) and D/D to RAF Bruggen for 14 Squadron as 'C'. Transferred to 226 OCU on 30/10/75, becoming code '18', and was repainted in the all-over wrap-around camouflage at 5 MU in 08/77. Upon return to the unit it subsequently crashed 14 miles west of Dingwall on 18/11/81 with the loss of the pilot.
XX759	S56 F/F 18/04/75 (E. Bucklow) and D/D RAF Bruggen 01/05/75 for 14 Squadron code 'D'. Re-assigned to 226 OCU 14/10/75 becoming code '19'. Repairs at 60 MU following a bird strike in 06/76, and repainted at 5 MU Kemble in 01/77. Returned to unit, and was the first aircraft to receive the revised unit markings, only to be lost in an accident on 01/11/78 near Selkirk.
XX760	S57 F/F 30/04/75 (P. Millett) and D/D to RAF Bruggen 22/05/75 for 14 Squadron as 'F'. Re-assigned to 226 OCU 20/11/76, taking code '26', and then to 5 MU for repainting as the first aircraft in the all-over wrap-around camouflage scheme, during 03/76. To 60 MU for overhaul and re-delivered to 14 Squadron as 'AA' in 12/76. The aircraft later crashed on 13/09/82, 2 miles north of Braegrudie on the Dalreavoch estate, Rogart, Sutherland. The pilot ejected safely.
XX761	S58 F/F 24/04/75 (E. Bucklow) and D/D to RAF Bruggen on 04/06/75 for No.14 Squadron, as 'G'. To 226 OCU on 18/11/75, taking the code '11', but was destroyed in a ground fire at RAF Lossiemouth after an engine explosion on 06/06/78. Remains used for ground instruction and the nose section was later reported at Warton, assigned maintenance serial 8600M. Later to Boscombe Down.
XX762	S59 F/F 14/05/75 (E. Bucklow) and D/D to RAF Bruggen on 04/06/75. Re-assigned to 226 OCU on 30/03/76, becoming code '28' with the unit. Repainted in all-over wrap-around camouflage at 5 MU in 05/76 but was later lost in a crash on 23/11/79, 200ft up on Chleibh, near Dalmally, Argyllshire, in which the pilot was killed.
XX763	S60 F/F 12/05/75 (E. Bucklow) and D/D to RAF Lossiemouth 26/06/75 for 226 OCU, code '24'. Repainted at 5 MU in all-over wrap-around camouflage in 03/77 and loaned to 54 Squadron in 01/80. Placed into store at RAF Shawbury by 04/85, and then assigned to ground instructional duties with No.4 SoTT at St Athan, now DARA Technical School, with maintenance serial 9009M.
XX764	S61 F/F 07/06/75 (E. Bucklow) and D/D to RAF Bruggen 02/07/75 for 14 Squadron as 'J'. Re-assigned to 226 OCU on 20/11/75, taking the code '27', and repainted in the all-over wrap-around camouflage at 5 MU during 04/76. Loaned to 6 Squadron during 11/88 and re-coded within 226 OCU to '13' before passing into store at RAF Shawbury on 03/09/84. Allocated to ground instructional duties with No.4 SoTT St Athan, now DARA Technical School, by 07/89, and assigned maintenance serial 9010M.
XX765	S62 F/F 13/06/75 (P. Ginger) and D/D to RAF Bruggen 02/07/75 for 14 Squadron but loaned to 17 Squadron before re-assignment to 226 OCU on 03/12/75 becoming code '27' with that unit. Repainted in the all-over wrap-around camouflage at 5 MU in 06/76, then placed in store with JMU. Bailed back to BAE SYSTEMS and flown to Warton on 04/08/78 by Eric Bucklow, to be fitted with the Dowty–Boulton Paul fly-by-wire system with a long-term project of a carbon fibre wing. F/F as FBW 20/10/81 with Chris Yeo at the controls, and with the aircraft sporting RAE red/white/blue corporate colours. F/F in its ACT (Active Control Technology) form with enlarged leading edge extensions on 15/03/84. Project completed and aircraft placed in store at Warton by 05/87. By 03/90 it had been repainted olive green and received the inscription 'ACT' in light blue on the fin. Stored again then transferred to RAF Cosford, and then back to Warton on 15/09/99. Currently preserved as part of the RAF Museum collection at RAF Cosford.
XX766	S63 F/F 14/06/75 (P. Ginger) and D/D to RAF Bruggen 08/07/75 for 17 Squadron. Re-assigned to 226 OCU on 18/12/75 taking the code '14'. Loaned to 54 Squadron for 'Red Flag' 02/80, upgraded to GR.1A at the JMU in 01/84, and re-issued to 54 Squadron as 'GP'. Transferred to 6 Squadron as 'EC' post-maintenance in 02/89, as a GR.1A. Later to receive '75th Anniversary' markings. Re-coded 'EA' by 05/90. Later received 'stage three' modifications including over-wing missile rails and Sky Guardian RWR. New grey colour scheme applied 09/95. To St Athan short-term store 01/98, and upgraded to GR.3 before issue to 16 (Reserve) Squadron as 'PE' on 31/05/01. Painted in special marks for 2001 display season and returned to St Athan for major overhaul on 10/09/04 and issued to 6 Squadron as 'EF' on 24/06/05.
XX767	S64 F/F 25/06/75 (E. Bucklow) and D/D to RAF Bruggen 18/05/75 for 14 Squadron. Re-assigned to 226 OCU on 29/10/75 becoming code '25' and repainted at 5 MU into all-over wrap-around camouflage during 03/77. Placed into short-term store at the JMU on 21/04/77 but then back to 14 Squadron as 'AU', changing to 'AN' by 07/79. Transferred to 31 Squadron as 'DC' by 09/83, to 17 Squadron as 'BD' by 10/84, and back to 226 OCU as '17' by 03/85. Upgraded to GR.1A at JMU and issued to 54 Squadron on 26/09/86, becoming code 'GE'. Had ARTF Arctic camouflage applied for Exercise Strong Resolve in 02/95, then received 'stage three' modifications and variously quoted as GR.1B or GR.1A(T). Received new grey colour scheme in 08/96 and upgraded to GR.3A at St Athan between 03/00 and 07/00. Served with 54 Squadron until disbandment and then re-assigned to 41 Squadron as 'FK' in 03/05. Flown to RAF Shawbury 11/04/06 for store.
XX768	S65 F/F 02/07/75 (E. Bucklow) and D/D to RAF Bruggen 12/08/75 for 14 Squadron. Transferred to 17 Squadron by 01/76, becoming code 'BA'. To 5 MU for painting into all-over wrap-around camouflage in 01/77, but crashed near to Heiesberg-Randerath on 29/09/82 following a rear-end fire.
XX817	S66 F/F 10/07/75 (J. Cockburn) and D/D to RAF Bruggen 20/08/75 for 17 Squadron. Coded 'BB' by 06/76 and received all-over wrap-around camouflage scheme at 5 MU in 03/77. Aircraft was lost on 17/07/80 when it crashed in woods 7 miles from Bruggen, with the pilot ejecting successfully.

The highly modified XX765 caught over Preston in formation with a Tornado F2 chase plane.

The first new Jaguar T.2 for No.54 (F) Squadron was XX829 delivered factory fresh on 23 December 1974. In common with most other twin-seaters it retained no allegiance, but its final operator was also No.54. It is captured here on 22 September 1999.

Delivered to Boscombe Down in 1985 following service with 226 OCU, XX830 was passed to the ETPS as a replacement for XX916 but was effectively retired in November 1996. It continued to be used for ground trials until disposed of in 2000. The cockpit section was saved by the Coltishall CRO to join his growing collection of artefacts.

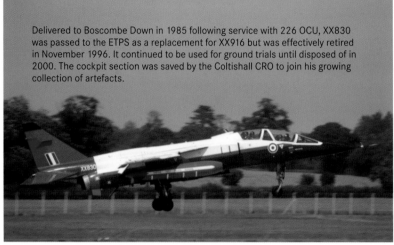

XX818	S67 F/F 10/07/75 (D. Eagles) and D/D to RAF Bruggen 15/08/75 for 17 Squadron. Coded 'BC' by 05/76 but transferred to 20 Squadron as 'CC' by 03/77 and then to 31 Squadron as 'DE' by 11/83. Returned to UK 02/11/84 for storage at RAF Shawbury and assigned to ground instructional duties with maintenance serial 8945M. Initially arriving at No.1 SoTT RAF Halton in 03/88, it moved to RAF Cosford, where it still resides today, following the closure of the former.
XX819	S68 F/F 05/08/75 (P. Ginger) and D/D to RAF Bruggen 20/08/75 for 17 Squadron. Assigned code 'BD', it was transferred to 20 Squadron by 11/78 to become 'CE'. Loaned to 226 OCU in 02/82, it was dispatched for storage at RAF Shawbury on 25/05/84 and assigned to ground instructional duties. Allocated maintenance serial 8923M, it was sent to No.2 SoTT RAF Cosford by 01/00, where it still resides today.
XX820	S69 F/F 13/08/75 (E. Bucklow) and D/D to RAF Bruggen 03/09/75 for 17 Squadron. Coded 'BE' by 06/76, it was transferred to 20 Squadron as 'CE' by 06/77 and back to 17 Squadron again by 11/78 as 'BD'. The aircraft crashed on 11/06/82, while being operated by 31 Squadron, when on final approach to RAF Bruggen, with the pilot ejecting safely.
XX821	S70 F/F 14/08/75 (A. Love) and D/D to RAF Bruggen 01/09/75 for 17 Squadron. Coded 'BF' by 06/76, it was transferred to 14 Squadron by 09/83, becoming code 'AN'. It was then re-assigned to 41 Squadron as 'P' by 03/85, passed into storage, and was then assigned to a ground instructional role, with maintenance serial 8896M, as part of the Servicing Instructional Flight (SIF) at RAF Cranwell on 30/07/86.
XX822	S71 F/F 29/08/75 (P. Millett) and D/D to RAF Bruggen 22/09/75 for 14 Squadron where it was assigned the code 'AA'. The aircraft crashed 15 miles north of Ahlhorn on 02/07/76.
XX823	S72 F/F 22/08/75 (A. Love) and D/D to RAF Bruggen 15/09/75 for 17 Squadron with code 'BG'. Aircraft crashed into a hill on 25/07/78 near Cagliari, Sardinia, while the unit was on APC at Decimomannu.
XX824	S73 F/F 02/09/75 (A. Love) and D/D to RAF Bruggen 23/09/75 for 14 Squadron as 'A'. Re-coded 'AB' before transfer to 17 Squadron by 09/78 as 'BH'. Re-assigned to 14 Squadron following overhaul at the JMU in late 1984, becoming code 'AD', but was retired to RAF Shawbury in 11/85 and assigned to ground instructional duties at RAF Halton by 01/90, with maintenance serial 9019M. Relocated to RAF Cosford when Halton closed. The jet is still current in the instructional role.
XX825	S74 F/F 14/09/75 (R. Stock) and D/D to RAF Bruggen 16/10/75 for 14 Squadron where it became code 'AC'. Transferred to 31 Squadron as 'DA' by 10/83 and then 17 Squadron as 'BN' by 10/84. It was then flown back to RAF Shawbury for storage. Allocated to the ground instructional role and assigned the maintenance serial 9020M, it was first used at No.1 SoTT RAF Halton, and then No.2 SoTT at RAF Cosford, where it resides today.

XX826	S75 F/F 12/09/75 (D. Eagles) and D/D to RAF Bruggen 16/10/75 for 14 Squadron. Initially coded 'B', this was altered to 'AD' by 06/76. Received all-over wrap-around camouflage at 5 MU in 11/76 the aircraft was re-assigned to 20 as 'CA' by 10/83, before passing to II (AC) Squadron in 07/84, taking up the code '34'. Flown to RAF Shawbury for storage on 05/03/85 and relegated to ground instructional use at RAF Cosford by 03/90. Assigned the maintenance serial 9021M, it still resides at Cosford today, although is up for disposal by tender through DSAT 3147 of 06/05.
XX827	S76 F/F 22/09/75 (A. Love) and D/D to RAF Bruggen 06/10/75 for 14 Squadron as code 'C'. Re-coded 'AE' by 06/76 and repainted in all-over wrap-around camouflage at 5 MU in 12/76. The aircraft was re-assigned to 20 Squadron as 'CL' on 08/03/77. Transferred to 17 Squadron as 'BM' by 09/78. It was lost in a crash over the Nellis Range on 12/02/81.
XX828	B16 F/F 07/10/74 (A. Love/P. Ginger) and used in FAV evaluation. D/D to RAF Lossiemouth 07/11/74 for 226 OCU as code 'P'. Crashed on 01/06/81, 5 miles north of Forfar. Both crew ejected safely.
XX829	B17 F/F 28/11/74 (D. Eagles/R. Taylor) and D/D to RAF Coltishall 23/12/74 for 54 Squadron. Coded 'GT' in 02/81, it was transferred to 6 Squadron as 'ER' by 01/85, then upgraded to T.2A. Loaned to 226 OCU in 02/86, it was back with 6 Squadron as 'ET' on 10/01/89, by which time it was sporting the legend 'Flying Can Openers' in red beneath the fin tip. Re-assigned to 16 (Reserve) Squadron as 'Y' by 03/94, then 54 Squadron as 'GZ' in 05/94, finally passing into store at RAF Shawbury on 06/03/01, where it resides today. It is up for disposal by tender DSAT 3146 of 26/05/05. Destined for D. Everett Aero, Sproughton.
XX830	B18 F/F 25/11/74 (E. Bucklow/R. Kenward) and D/D to RAF Lossiemouth 20/12/74 for 226 OCU as code 'R'. Loaned to A&AEE in 04/85 then, following overhaul at the JMU in 11/86, was transferred permanently to the ETPS. Placed in store at St Athan in 11/96 then Shawbury in 02/99. The fuselage was taken by road to Warton on 29/09/99 for T.2A upgrade development. Following this it was removed, once again by road, to RAF Coltishall on 06/07/00, where the cockpit was preserved and the fuselage was moved onward to Bruntingthorpe for component reclamation and then scrapped. Assigned maintenance serial 9293M.
XX831	B19 F/F 10/12/74 (A. Love/V. Malings) and used on flights six through twenty-three on flameout investigations. D/D to RAF Lossiemouth 21/03/75 for 226OCU, code 'W', but crashed shortly afterwards on 30/04/75.

XX832 is currently preserved at Bentwaters, the former USAFE base, following a period in store at Shawbury between 2001 and 2005.

XX832	B20 F/F 16/12/74 (A. Love/V. Malings) and D/D to RAF Lossiemouth 03/02/75 for 226 OCU as code 'S'. Remained with unit until placed in short-term store at RAF Shawbury in 01/91. Following overhaul at St Athan on 12/05/95 the aircraft, now sporting the new grey colour scheme, was assigned to 16 (Reserve) Squadron, code 'Z'. Transferred to 6 Squadron as 'EZ' by 09/99 as a T.2A. It reportedly suffered an in-flight collision with XX745, which necessitated another visit to St Athan on 13/07/00. Returning to Coltishall on 16/02/01, it was flown to RAF Shawbury for storage on 12/10/01, where it resides today. It is up for disposal by tender through DSAT 3146 of 26/05/05. Destined for D. Everett Aero, Sproughton, but put on display at former USAFE base at Bentwaters.
XX833	B21 F/F 17/01/75 (E. Bucklow/R. Kenward) and D/D to RAF Lossiemouth 21/02/75 for 226 OCU, code 'T'. Transferred to 20 Squadron as 'CZ' by early 1977, before passing on to 14 Squadron as 'AZ' in 04/84. Upgraded to T.2A and re-issued to 41 Squadron as 'Z' by 06/86 it was initially loaned then permanently assigned to 'A' Flight RAE Farnborough. Noted wearing the code 'N2' in 05/89 and the CTTO badge in 01/90 it had, by then, been transferred to the DRA Experimental Flying Squadron at Boscombe Down as the TIALD research aircraft. Named 'Night Cat' and re-designated T.2B (or possibly T.2A(T)) it has remained with QinetiQ. During overhaul at St Athan in 09/96, it received the new grey colour scheme.
XX834	B22 F/F 05/02/75 (A. Love/R. Stock) and D/D RAF Lossiemouth 17/03/75 for 226 OCU, code 'U'. Transferred to 14 Squadron as 'AY' by 10/78, although back with 226 OCU shortly afterwards. By 08/84 it had been re-issued to II (AC) Squadron as '37', then re-coded '34' by 05/85, finally transferring to 6 Squadron as 'EZ'. It was here that it was lost in a crash on 07/08/88, when it struck high-tension wires near Wildbad-Kreuth, West Germany, with the loss of the pilot, although the USAF back-seater ejected safely.
XX835	B23 F/F 14/02/75 (E. Bucklow/J. Evans) and D/D to RAF Lossiemouth 17/03/75 for 226 OCU, code 'V'. Loaned to RAE in 09/86 and upgraded to T.2B, it was re-issued to 54 Squadron on 10/10/95 with spells on 6 Squadron and 41 Squadron as 'FY'. It was flown to St Athan on 23/08/99 for upgrade to T.4, returning to 41 Squadron afterwards. It is now assigned to 6 Squadron as 'EX'.
XX836	B24 F/F 08/03/75 (J. Cockburn/R. Woollett) and D/D 27/03/75 to RAF Coltishall for 54 Squadron, but destined for 14 Squadron, to whom it was re-delivered on 07/04/75. Coded 'AZ', it was transferred to 17 Squadron as 'BZ' on 28/08/80 then, following upgrade to T.2A at the JMU on 18/10/85, it was re-issued to 6 Squadron as 'ER'. It served with the unit until at least 1989, when the jet was relocated to RAF Shawbury for long-term store. It remained at Shawbury from at least 08/89, until 10/08/05 when it was sold to D. Everett, Sproughton, Suffolk, following sale by tender DSAT 3146 of 26/05/05.
XX837	B25 F/F 21/03/75 (T. Ferguson/R. Stock) and D/D to RAF Lossiemouth 23/05/75 for 226 OCU as code 'Z'. Placed in store at RAF Shawbury by 07/86 and then identified for ground instructional duties at No.1 SoTT at RAF Halton, where it arrived by 06/89. Assigned maintenance serial 8978M, it relocated to RAF Cosford, where it resides today, coded 'I', following the closure of Halton.
XX838	B26 F/F 05/04/75 (E. Bucklow/R. Stock) and D/D to RAF Lossiemouth 29/04/75 for 226 OCU, code 'X'. Loaned to 17 Squadron 01/12/75 until 16/01/76, then to 60 MU for overhaul, before returning to 226 OCU. Delivered to Warton 16/05/78 for evaluation by FAV, including Brig.- Gen. Bracho. Returned to Lossiemouth 19/05/78. Placed in short-term store at RAF Shawbury by 09/91, until 30/06/98 when it was dispatched to St Athan for T.4 upgrade, following which, on 05/05/99, it was re-issued to 16 (Reserve) Squadron as 'R' and on moving to RAF Coltishall 'PR'. At demise of unit, it was assigned to 41 Squadron in 03/05 as 'FZ'. Noted sporting a Union Jack and motif – 'Jaguar Display 2005' – on fin, but this was short-lived. Wfu St Athan by 03/06.
XX839	B27 F/F 18/04/75 (T. Ferguson/R. Woollett) and D/D to RAF Lossiemouth 22/05/75 for 226 OCU as 'Y'. To RAF Shawbury for a short period in store between 07/86 and 05/88. Following overhaul at the JMU, it returned to its original unit. Assigned to 54 Squadron as 'GW' by 04/95, but was found while on major overhaul to have structural problems, and was retired to ground instructional duties after 10/95. Assigned maintenance serial 9256M, it was used by the DARA Civilian Technical Training School (CTTS) at St Athan until 05/02, when it was sold as scrap to Conifer Metals, Clay Cross, Chesterfield.

Operated by Squadron Nos II (AC), 6, 16, 41 and 54, XX842 has been modified to Jaguar T.4, and received the Adour 106 engine upgrade, indicating that it will probably be one the last twin-seaters in the inventory.

XX840	B28 F/F 17/05/75 (E. Bucklow/R. Stock) and D/D to RAF Bruggen on 12/06/75 for 17 Squadron as code 'BZ'. Re-assigned to 226 OCU as 'A' by 09/80 and, following T.2A upgrade at the JMU, was issued in 02/88 to II (AC) Squadron as '34', then '33', and finally, on demise of that unit, to 41 Squadron as 'X' on 27/01/89. Placed in short-term store at RAF Shawbury by 10/90. It remained in store until it was transferred to St Athan on 24/09/98 for T.4 upgrade. It was not immediately re-issued to service but assigned to 16 (Reserve) Squadron in 05/99 as 'S', then re-coded 'PS', until allocated to 6 Squadron as 'EY' following the former's disbandment. Flown to St Athan 29/03/06 for store.
XX841	B29 F/F 16/05/75 (P. Ginger/V. Malings) and displayed at Paris Salon on 30/05/75, returning to Warton 09/06/75. D/D to RAF Lossiemouth 27/06/75 for 226OCU, code 'K'. Re-assigned to 41 Squadron as 'S' by 04/85. It then spent a short period in store at RAF Shawbury from 05/86 to early 1990, following which it was loaned to the ETPS. Transferred to 6 Squadron as 'ES' by 06/92, then upgraded at St Athan to T.4 in 10/99, emerging in the new grey colour scheme. Moved to 16 (Reserve) Squadron as 'PQ' by 02/02, where it stayed until the squadron's disbandment. It was then allocated to 6 Squadron as 'EW'.
XX842	B30 F/F 04/06/75 (E. Bucklow/J. Evans) and D/D to RAF Lossiemouth 30/06/75 for 226 OCU as code 'W'. To 54 Squadron on 31/07/75 and then 41 Squadron as 'T' by 09/76, it was transferred to II (AC) Squadron following overhaul at the JMU in late 1986 as '33'. It then returned to Coltishall, this time with 6 Squadron as 'EW', in 10/88, although it spent a period on loan to both the ETPS and RAE at Farnborough between 23/02/89 and 12/06/90. Sent for short-term store at RAF Shawbury in 08/94, it was re-issued to 41 Squadron as 'FV' on 08/07/96, following repainting into the new grey scheme. Re-assigned to 16 (Reserve) Squadron as 'X', then upgraded to T.4 at St Athan in 10/00. It was then loaned to Warton as part of the Rolls–Royce Adour engine upgrade programme, returning to Coltishall 31/10/02 initially to 16 (Reserve) Squadron then, on its disbandment, to 41 Squadron as 'FX'. Wfu St Athan by 03/06.
XX843	B31 F/F 24/06/75 (T. Ferguson/R. Taylor) and D/D to RAF Lossiemouth 18/07/75 for 226 OCU, code 'W'. Re-issued to II (AC) Squadron as 'T' by 05/76. It was subsequently re-coded '33', then '36', before returning to JMU on 03/01/85 for T.2A upgrade. Loaned to 226 OCU as 'E' in 02/86. It was re-assigned to 54 Squadron as 'GT' in 08/87 but crashed on 29/08/91 following a mid-air collision with a Cessna 152 over Carno, near Newtown, Powys. The two crew ejected, but the rear-seater, an RAF Wing Commander who had just returned to limited flying following a lung/heart transplant, was killed, as was the pilot of the Cessna.

XX844	B32 F/F 05/08/75 (R. Stock/R. Woollett) and D/D to RAF Bruggen 27/08/75 for use by 31 Squadron, code 'DZ'. Transferred to 17 Squadron as 'BY' by 12/83, then to 226 OCU as 'F' by 04/85. It was then loaned to the A&AEE at Boscombe Down in 07/87, followed by a period with the Cranfield CIT in 01/90. The aircraft was then identified for ground instructional training and allocated the maintenance serial 9023M, for use by No.2 SoTT at RAF Cosford, where it arrived in 03/90. By 01/98, it had been returned to St Athan for spares recovery.
XX845	B33 F/F 12/08/75 (J. Cockburn/Krautlann (MBB pilot)) and D/D to RAF Bruggen 27/08/75 for 17 Squadron, code 'BY'. Transferred to 20 Squadron 'CZ' by 03/77 and then II (AC) Squadron in 07/77, where it was damaged on landing on 16/11/77. Taken to 431 MU for repairs, it returned to flying status on 09/04/79, returning to II (AC) Squadron as '34'. Following periods of use with 17 Squadron as 'BY' and 14 Squadron as 'AZ', as well as 226 OCU, it was re-assigned to 41 Squadron as 'V' on 07/02/89. Transferred to 226 OCU as 'A' in 09/93, it returned to Coltishall for 6 Squadron in 06/94, becoming 'ET'. Upgraded to T.4 at St Athan in the 03/05 re-shuffle, it was assigned the code 'EV', but was flown to St Athan on 01/06/05 for spares recovery.
XX846	B34 F/F 21/08/75 (J. Cockburn/R. Kenward) but held by the company to undertake Middle East sales tour between 13/11/75 and 13/12/75. Fitted with Dash-26 engines, it undertook its F/F in the new configuration on 04/11/75. Returned to Warton to undertake a series of demonstration flights, involving IAF pilot Air Vice Marshal Zaheer. Normal engines were refitted and the aircraft was test flown 28/01/76, then D/D to RAF Lossiemouth 14/03/76 for 226 OCU as 'A'. It was re-assigned to 14 Squadron as 'AZ' for a short period, before returning to its former position with the OCU. Incurred a nose wheel collapse on landing at RAF Lossiemouth 29/11/84. It had returned to flying by 01/85 and was then upgraded to T.2A in 09/87. Loaned to the RAE on 23/11/87, before re-assignment as 41 Squadron 'Y' in 08/88. Another period of loan with ETPS took place in early 02/89 followed, by a short period of store at RAF Shawbury from 27/02/89 until 09/90 when it was overhauled at the JMU. Once again assigned to 226 OCU as 'A' in 05/92 it was issued to 41 Squadron as 'FY' by 07/93, then 16 (Reserve) Squadron as 'V' in 02/95, before re-coding to 'PV' in 06/01. It was wfu by 08/04, and broken up for spares by 24/08/05. Remains departed Coltishall 20/02/06.
XX847	B35 F/F 23/10/75 (E. Bucklow/J. Evans) and D/D to RAF Lossiemouth 10/11/75 for 226 OCU code 'Q'. To II (AC) Squadron by 06/76, then 14 Squadron as 'AY' in 07/86. Sent for overhaul at JMU 19/01/80, becoming the 100th Jaguar to undergo overhaul with the unit. Returned to 14 Squadron 01/07/80 but transferred to 20 Squadron as 'CZ' by 04/84 and then to 31 Squadron as 'DY' on 20/07/84. Returned to UK in 10/84 and had been re-issued to 226 OCU as 'G' by 03/85. Placed in short-term store at RAF Shawbury by 07/86, it remained there until returning to the JMU for upgrade in 05/90. Transferred to 41 Squadron as 'X' by 04/91, then 'FX' in 03/95. It was dispatched to St Athan by road for storage on 08/12/95. Participated in the Jaguar fatigue test programme then upgraded to T.4, which included the fitting of the upgraded Adour 106 engine. F/F in this configuration 26/06/02. It was delivered to 16 (Reserve) Squadron in 10/02 as 'PY', before being allocated to 6 Squadron as 'EZ' in 03/05.

XX846 'A' of 226 OCU is prepared for flight on 16 September 1996.

Now no longer in service XX845, coded 'ET', is seen in
formation with XZ361 'T' of No.41 Squadron.

Once wearing the 'Fat Slags' nose art, XX962 is seen here in earlier days in the service of No.20 Squadron when visiting RAF Coningsby on 25 March 1982.

XX915	B36 F/F 22/06/76 (A. Love/R. Stock) and used for evaluation by Nigerian AF and D/D 20/07/76 to ETPS at Boscombe Down. Borrowed for 1976 SBAC show and flown by Canadian and Turkish AF pilots. Returned to Boscombe Down 14/10/76 but borrowed again on 10/03/78 for further Indian Air Force evaluation. Lost in a crash on 17/01/84 near to Porton Down, Wiltshire, with the pilot ejecting safely.
XX916	B37 F/F 02/12/76 (A. Love/R. Kenward) and D/D 18/01/77 to ETPS at Boscombe Down. Lost in a crash on 17/07/81 into Bristol Channel off Hartland Point. Both crew ejected, but one was killed.
XX955	S77 F/F 18/09/75 (A. Love) and D/D to RAF Bruggen 06/10/75 for 14 Squadron, coded 'AF' by 03/76. Repainted in wrap-around camouflage at 5 MU in 03/77, and re-issued to 17 Squadron as 'BC' by 10/83. It returned to 14 Squadron as 'AN' by 10/84, then transferred to 54 Squadron in 10/85, becoming code 'GM'. Upgraded to GR.1A at JMU in 11/86 and returned to 54 Squadron as 'GK'. Sent for storage at RAF Shawbury by 10/98, where it remained until sold by tender DSAT 3146 of 26/05/05 to the museum at Hermeskiel, Germany. The airframe departed Shawbury 06/09/05 via D. Everett Aero, Sproughton, but had arrived at the German museum by early October.
XX956	S78 F/F 26/09/75 (A. Love) and D/D to RAF Bruggen 22/10/75 for 17 Squadron, receiving code 'BH' by 03/76. Repainted in all-over wrap-around camouflage at 5 MU in 11/76, it was transferred briefly to 14 Squadron as 'AB' in 10/78, but was back with 17 Squadron by 03/79. Transferred to 31 Squadron as 'DK' by 08/84, it then returned yet again to 17 Squadron as 'BE' by 10/84. Delivered to RAF Shawbury 28/02/85 for store, and identified for ground instructional training. Allocated maintenance serial 8950M for use by No.1 SoTT at RAF Halton where it had arrived by 03/88. Transferred to RAF Cosford, where it still resides, upon closure of Halton.
XX957	S79 F/F 03/10/75 (R. Stock) and D/D to RAF Bruggen 24/10/75 for 14 Squadron, taking up the code 'AG' by 06/76. Transferred to 20 Squadron as 'CG' by 03/77, but crashed on approach to Bruggen on 21/10/81 after being struck by lightning.
XX958	S80 F/F 07/10/75 (E. Bucklow) and D/D to RAF Bruggen 24/10/75 for use by 14 Squadron. Coded 'AH' by 05/76. Noted sporting an ARTF Arctic colour scheme in 01/80. Transferred to 17 Squadron as 'BK' by 12/83. It was flown to RAF Shawbury on 12/03/85 for storage and then allocated to ground instructional duties as 9022M, arriving by 03/90 at No.2 SoTT RAF Cosford, where it still resides today.
XX959	S81 F/F 14/10/75 (A. Love) and D/D to RAF Bruggen 04/11/75 for 14 Squadron, adopting code 'AJ' by 06/76. Transferred to 20 Squadron as 'CJ' by 06/77 and flown to RAF Shawbury for storage on 04/07/84. Allocated to ground instructional duties with maintenance serial 8959M, arriving by 03/88 at No.2 SoTT RAF Cosford, where it resides today.
XX960	S82 F/F 18/10/75 (E. Bucklow) and D/D to RAF Bruggen 03/11/75 for 14 Squadron, receiving code 'AK' by 03/76. Crashed on 18/07/79 near Iserlohn, West Germany, with the pilot ejecting safely.
XX961	S83 F/F 20/10/75 (A. Love) and D/D to RAF Bruggen 10/11/75 for 17 Squadron, where it had taken the code 'BJ' by 0676. Lost in a crash on 28/05/80 following a collision with XX964 near Bruggen.
XX962	S84 F/F 30/10/75 (E. Bucklow) and D/D to RAF Bruggen 13/11/75 for 17 Squadron, receiving code 'BK' by 06/76. Transferred to 20 Squadron as 'CK' by 05/77, but back with 17 Squadron as 'BU' in 11/78 and 'BG' in 11/83. Relocated to Coltishall and 6 Squadron as 'EK' by 08/86. Upgraded for Gulf operations and repainted in desert pink ARTF before deploying to Thumrait on 02/11/90. Coded 'X', it received the 'Fat Slags' nose art and thirty-seven mission symbols. Returned to UK 13/03/91 and repainted into normal scheme by 06/91 as 'EK'. Sent to Boscombe Down as one of the first three aircraft to receive TIALD modifications in 02/95 which, together with the 'stage three' modifications previously received, saw its designation change to GR.1B. Participated in Operation Deliberate Force in 1995 sporting the grey (baby blue) ARTF scheme and, during which, it had five mission symbols applied. Lost its temporary colours by 12/95 and six months later was placed in store at Coltishall, pending disposal. Dispatched to the Aircraft Maintenance Instruction Flight at RAF Cranwell then later, by 07/02, to No.1 SoTT at RAF Cosford, coded 'P', and wearing maintenance serial 9257M.
XX963	S85 F/F 18/11/75 (J. Cockburn) and D/D to RAF Bruggen 02/12/75 for 14 Squadron, receiving the code 'AL' by 03/76. Lost in a crash on 25/05/82 near Wesel, West Germany, after an internal explosion caused by a strike by an AIM-9 Sidewinder missile fired accidentally by No.92 Squadron Phantom FGR.2 XV422 'O'. Pilot ejected safely.
XX964	S86 F/F 11/11/75 (D. Eagles) and D/D to RAF Bruggen 27/11/75 for 17 Squadron, receiving the code 'BL' by 06/76. Lost following the collision with XX961 on 28/05/80.
XX965	S87 F/F 06/11/75 (E. Bucklow) and D/D to RAF Bruggen 21/11/75 for 14 Squadron receiving code 'AM' by 06/76. Upgraded to GR.1A at JMU in 1983 and re-issued to 54 Squadron as 'GB' 08/84. Transferred to 226 OCU as '04' on 06/03/86, changing code to '07' in 1992 when it was used as the 1993 Jaguar display aircraft. On 226 OCU becoming 16 (Reserve) Squadron in 03/94, it took the code 'C', and was then placed into store at RAF Coltishall during 01/86 and passed to the Aircraft Maintenance Instruction Flight at RAF Cranwell, where it still resides, as 9254M.
XX966	S88 F/F 19/11/75 (D. Eagles) and D/D to RAF Bruggen 02/12/75 for 17 Squadron coded 'BM' by 06/76. Transferred to 20 Squadron as 'CL' by 09/78. Loaned for a short period to A&AEE, before returning to 20 Squadron on 27/10/80 as 'CD'. Upgrade to GR.1A followed with re-issue to 54 Squadron as 'GK' in 08/84, passing on to 6 Squadron as 'EL' by 04/85. Sent for storage at RAF Shawbury on 18/09/85 and assigned to ground instructional training at No.1 SoTT as 8904M by 12/86. Following the closure of RAF Halton the airframe was relocated to RAF Cosford, after being displayed at Earls Court in 08/98. It arrived at Cosford shortly afterwards, where it still resides, coded 'J'.
XX967	S89 F/F 24/11/75 (A. Love) and undertook trials to prove modification to brake chute handle. D/D to RAF Bruggen 15/01/76 for 31 Squadron, where it was coded 'DA' by 05/76. Transferred to 14 Squadron as 'AC' by 10/83. It was flown to storage at RAF Shawbury by 11/87 and then assigned to ground instructional training as 9006M, arriving by 07/89 at RAF Cosford, where it is still in use today.
XX968	S90 F/F 24/11/75 (E. Bucklow) and D/D to RAF Bruggen for 31 Squadron, becoming 'DB' by 06/76. Transferred to 14 Squadron as 'AJ' by 12/83. It was retired to RAF Shawbury in 11/87 and allocated to the ground instructional role at RAF Cosford. Assigned the maintenance serial 9007M it had arrived by 07/89 at Cosford, where it still resides today.
XX969	S91 F/F 01/12/75 (A. Love) and D/D to RAF Bruggen on 06/01/76 for 31 Squadron, receiving code 'DC' by 06/76. Transferred to 226 OCU on 14/11/83, taking up the code '01', it was retired by 08/96 to the ground instructional role as 8897M at RAF Cosford, where it is still current today.

Jaguar GR.1 XX967 'DA', No.31 Squadron, outside one of Bruggen's hardened aircraft shelters (HAS).

In its short ten-year operational history XX975, seen here as 'DJ' of No.31 Squadron, went on to serve with 17 Squadron and 226 OCU before being assigned to ground instructional training.

| XX970 | S92 F/F 08/12/75 (J. Lee) and D/D to RAF Bruggen 06/01/76 for 31 Squadron where, by 06/76, it had taken up the code 'DD'. Suffered a landing mishap in 1982 and was passed to 431 MU for repairs. Re-issued to 17 Squadron as 'BJ' by 10/84 and then to 226 OCU as '11' by 04/85, before moving to 6 Squadron on 28/01/86. Coded 'EH', it was to be sent to the Gulf in the first cadre of aircraft for Operation Granby. As a consequence it received the desert pink ARTF scheme in 08/90 but had returned to the UK before hostilities began. Received 'stage three' modifications and was painted in ARTF grey in 06/93 for UN peacekeeping duties and was upgraded to GR.1B standard at St Athan between 13/10/95 and 22/01/96. Repainted in the new grey colour scheme in 08/96, it has remained with 6 Squadron as 'EH' ever since, and was later upgraded to GR.3A in 01/02. |

XX971	S93 F/F 11/12/75 (R. Stock) and D/D to RAF Bruggen 06/01/76 for 31 Squadron, taking the code 'DE' by 06/76. Repainted in all-over wrap-around camouflage at 5 MU in 11/76, it was lost in a crash at Lahr, West Germany, on 21/03/78. The fuselage was recovered and dispatched to the AWRE at the PEE, Shoeburyness, by 12/79, and was still extant two years later.
XX972	S94 F/F 12/12/75 (E. Bucklow) and D/D to RAF Bruggen 06/01/76 for 31 Squadron, adopting the code 'DF' by 06/76. Lost in a crash at Barnard Castle, Co. Durham, during Exercise Osex 4 on 14/04/81, with the pilot being killed.
XX973	S95 F/F 05/01/76 (E. Bucklow) and D/D to RAF Bruggen 15/01/76 for 31 Squadron, adopting code 'DG' by 06/76. Lost in a crash 4 miles south-west of Gutersloh, West Germany, on 14/04/81, with the pilot ejecting safely.
XX974	S96 F/F 09/01/76 (E. Bucklow) and D/D to RAF Bruggen 28/01/76 for 31 Squadron, where it had taken the code 'DH' by 06/76. Returned to UK on 26/10/84 and, following overhaul, was issued to 6 Squadron as 'EG'. It was upgraded to GR.1A at JMU in 04/87, and then returned to 6 Squadron. The aircraft was part of the first batch of Jaguars to head for the Gulf in 08/90. It received the ARTF desert pink colour scheme but returned before hostilities began. Repainted by 06/91, it was later transferred to 54 Squadron by 01/92 as 'GH'. Received grey ARTF finish in 06/93 for UN peacekeeping duties and again in 06/94, by which time it had received the 'stage three' modifications. Re-assigned to 16 (Reserve) Squadron as 'B' in 1993, by which time it had become a GR.3. Recoded 'PB' by 02/01, upgraded at St Athan to GR.3A in 11/01, and transferred to 41 Squadron as 'FE' by 03/03 when, once again, it received the ARTF finish. It was dispatched by road to St Athan 16/12/04, where it was wfu. Departed to D.Everett Aero, Sproughton.
XX975	S97 F/F 12/01/76 (E. Bucklow) and fitted with rain erosion strips on leading edges of wings and tailplane. Used on UHF radio trial, D/D to Boscombe Down 30/01/76 for use by 'A' Squadron. D/D to 31 Squadron 28/05/76, becoming 'DJ' by 06/76. Transferred to 17 Squadron as 'BA' by 01/84 and then to 226 OCU as '07' by 04/85. Flown to RAF Shawbury for storage by 03/86, and assigned to ground instructional training at No.1 SoTT RAF Halton as 8905M, delivered by 12/86. On closure of the unit, the aircraft transferred to RAF Cosford, where it still resides today.
XX976	S98 F/F 13/01/76 (E. Bucklow) and D/D to RAF Bruggen 28/01/76 for 31 Squadron. Coded 'DK' by 06/76, it was transferred to 17 Squadron as 'BD' by 06/84, before being retired to RAF Shawbury on 12/03/85. Assigned to ground instructional duties at No.1 SoTT by 12/86. It took the maintenance serial 8906M. On closure of the unit, the aircraft transferred to RAF Cosford, where it resides today.
XX977	S99 F/F 20/01/76 (E. Bucklow) and D/D to RAF Bruggen 20/02/76 for 31 Squadron. Coded 'DL' by 06/76, it incurred a bird strike in late 04/78, necessitating attention by 431 MU. Flying again on 15/01/79, it next had an in-flight emergency after it had clipped a tower at Charwelton, near Northampton. The aircraft made an emergency landing at RAE Thurleigh, having suffered damage to port wing and external tank. Taken by road to RAF Shawbury on 06/12/84, it was placed in store until assigned to ground instructional training on 06/12/91. Initially destined to RAF Abingdon for BDR training it was re-allocated to the Aircraft Recovery and Transportation Flight at St Athan, where it still resides.
XX978	S100 F/F 22/01/76 (P. Ginger) and D/D to RAF Bruggen 25/02/76 for 31 Squadron, taking the code 'DM' by 06/76. Aircraft lost in a crash on 14/06/77 near to Verden, West Germany.
XX979	S101 F/F 27/01/76 (E. Bucklow) and D/D to Boscombe Down 11/02/76 for use by 'A' Squadron A&AEE. Demonstrated to President of Romania at Filton 15/06/78 and returned to Warton for EMC checks 24/01/79. Delivered to Farnborough 30/08/80. Upgraded to GR.1A standard, it was delivered to St Athan for storage in 09/99, where it remained until taken by road to RAF Coltishall on 19/02/02. Allocated the maintenance serial 9306M, the forward fuselage was used as a ground procedures trainer. In 09/05 it was being used for spares recovery prior to disposal.

XZ101	S102 F/F 04/02/76 (P. Ginger) and originally incorrectly assigned the serial XY101. D/D to RAF Laarbruch 26/02/76 for II (AC) Squadron, where it took the code letter 'S'. Repainted in the all-over wrap-around colour scheme at 5 MU in 10/76, it was later re-coded '21' in 08/81 and then transferred to 17 Squadron in 08/82 as 'BD'. It then returned to II (AC) Squadron on 10/07/84 as a GR.1A, coded '20'. Returned to the UK on 07/05/86 and assigned to 41 Squadron as 'Q', becoming the first GR.1A for that unit. Remained on strength until early 1993 when transferred to 226 OCU as '06', then 16 (Reserve) Squadron as 'D' in 03/94. Placed in store at RAF Coltishall in 07/96 it was relegated to ground instructional duties as 9282M at Boscombe Down.
XZ102	S103 F/F 11/02/76 (A. Love) and originally incorrectly assigned the serial XY102. D/D RAF Laarbruch 05/03/76 for II (AC) Squadron, code 'H'. Lost in a crash on 14/12/76, 10 km north-east of Laarbruch.
XZ103	S104 F/F 16/02/76 (E. Bucklow) and originally incorrectly assigned the serial XY103. D/D to RAF Laarbruch 27/02/76 for II (AC) Squadron as code 'I'. Re-coded '23' by 08/80 and upgraded to GR.1A on 03/01/85. Returned to JMU, then, after a brief period in store at RAF Shawbury between 11/90 and 06/92, it was re-issued to 41 Squadron as 'P'. Received an Arctic ARTF scheme in 02/95 for participation in Exercise Strong Resolve. Upgraded to Jaguar 96 configuration at St Athan between 18/05/98 and 27/08/98. Returning to 41 Squadron, it was coded 'FP'. On 23/11/98, following a multiple bird strike over Herburn, the pilot had to make an emergency landing at Newcastle Airport with one engine shut down and an insecure external tank. Aircraft departed by road to St Athan for repairs but returned to service in 01/00, by which time it had been re-designated GR.3A. Loaned to SAOEU in early 1992 to participate in the annual series of trials held at China Lake NWC. One of these was 'Trial Flashman', for which, along with Tornado GR.4 ZD792, it was painted in a mixed ARTF scheme of grey body and undersides and desert pink upper surfaces. Alas it went 'technical' just prior to departure and was replaced by XZ109 in normal grey scheme. Special scheme removed by 05/92 and, in 2005, it became the season's Jaguar display platform with No.41 Squadron.
XZ104	S105 F/F 25/02/76 (J.J. Lee) and originally incorrectly assigned the serial XY104. D/D to RAF Laarbruch 11/03/76 for II (AC) Squadron as code 'N'. Flown from JMU to Warton 18/03/80 for radio trials in conjunction with RAE Farnborough. Re-coded '24', the aircraft was selected to receive the unit's special '75th Anniversary' marks during 05/88. Transferred to 6 Squadron on 12/01/89, it was one of the first aircraft to receive the ARTF desert pink scheme in 03/89 for a deployment to the Canary Islands. Transferred to 41 Squadron as 'M', it again received the desert pink ARTF as a spare aircraft for Operation Granby with the code 'FM'. The aircraft was to receive the 'stage three' modifications, and participated in a number of UN peacekeeping operations, sporting the grey ARTF. Upgraded to GR.1A and loaned to the SAOEU in 08/96, the aircraft remains on 41 Squadron strength as 'FM'.
XZ105	S106 F/F 13/02/76 (E. Bucklow) and originally incorrectly assigned the serial XY105. D/D to RAF Laarbruch 05/03/76 for II (AC) Squadron as 'Y'. Re-coded '25' by 08/80, it was lost in a crash near to CFB Goose Bay on 16/06/83, following a collision with XZ110.
XZ106	S107 F/F 23/02/76 (E. Bucklow) and originally incorrectly assigned the serial XY106. D/D to RAF Laarbruch 05/03/76 for II (AC) Squadron as code 'E'. Re-coded '26' by 08/80 and upgraded to GR.1A by 08/84. Flown to RAF Shawbury by way of Coltishall on 11/01/89 for a period of short-term store before delivery to JMU in 08/90 for Gulf War modifications and repainting in ARTF desert pink. Flew to Thumrait 06/12/90, received the 'Girl with the Union Jack' nose art, code 'O', and thirty-five mission symbols. Returned to UK on 13/03/91 to 41 Squadron as 'FR' but retained the desert pink scheme. It was then dispatched to Incirlik as part of Operation Warden on 04/09/91, a duty it continued to undertake due to its 'stage three' modifications. Loaned to the AWC/SAOEU at Boscombe Down in 11/95, it was re-designated GR.1B or GR.1B(R). Sent to St Athan on 08/02/02 for overhaul and GR.3A upgrade. Returned to 41 Squadron 12/12/02 and was repainted in ARTF Arctic camouflage for the annual deployment to Bardufoss. Assigned the code 'FW' in the shuffle after the disbanding of 16 and 54 Squadron, but at St Athan in 07/05 for spares recovery.
XZ107	S108 F/F 05/03/76 (E. Bucklow) and originally incorrectly assigned the serial XY107. D/D to RAF Laarbruch 18/03/76 for II (AC) Squadron as 'R'. Re-coded '27' then transferred to 6 Squadron as 'EN' by 12/82 and on to 41 Squadron as 'H' by 11/83. Received Arctic camouflage scheme for deployment to Bardufoss between 05/03/88 and 18/03/88 and again in 02/96 for Exercise Battle Griffin. Upgraded to GR.3 in mid-1997 and GR.3A in 11/03, it remained on 41 Squadron strength as 'FH' until wfu St Athan by 03/06.
XZ108	S109 F/F 03/03/76 (J.J. Lee) and originally incorrectly assigned the serial XY108. First aircraft to receive factory-finish wrap-around camouflage. Undertook radio trials with XX975. D/D to RAF Laarbruch 09/06/76 for II (AC) Squadron as code 'W'. Involved in a landing mishap at De Peel in 1978 and dispatched to 431 MU for repairs. Returned to squadron 24/08/79 and re-coded '28'. Upgraded to GR.1A by 08/84 and transferred to 54 Squadron as 'GD' on 05/01/89. Involved in a collision with Tornado GR.1A ZA394 'I' of II (AC) Squadron over Hexham, Northumberland, on 09/01/90. The Jaguar recovered with approximately 1 m of wing missing but the Tornado crashed, with the crew ejecting safely. Repaired at JMU and returned to squadron, but re-assigned to 16 (Reserve) Squadron by 02/94 and coded 'E'. Loaned to A&AEE in 02/95 and received new grey colour scheme at JMU in 06/95. Returned to 16 (Reserve) Squadron, this time as 'A'. Back with 54 Squadron 08/08/96 as 'GL' before upgrade to Jaguar 96 configuration at St Athan in 01/98. The aircraft was lost in a crash on 03/09/98, approximately 12 miles off the Norfolk coast, during ACM. The pilot ejected safely.
XZ109	S110 F/F 16/03/76 (P. Ginger) and originally incorrectly assigned serial XY109. D/D 02/04/76 to RAF Laarbruch for II (AC) Squadron as 'O'. Re-coded '29' by 08/80 and upgraded at JMU to GR.1A in 10/84. Transferred to RAF Coltishall on 16/12/88 and, after overhaul with the JMU, assigned to 54 Squadron as 'GL' on 13/04/89. Received desert pink ARTF scheme and deployed to Incirlik under Operation Warden on 09/09/91. It was transferred to 6 Squadron as 'EN' by 03/93 and, having received the 'stage three' modifications, was used extensively on UN peacekeeping operations in the ARTF grey scheme. Received new permanent grey scheme in 10/95 and was then upgraded to GR.3 in late 1998 and GR.3A in 03/03, when it was loaned to the SAOEU. However, it still remains on 6 Squadron strength as 'EN'.
XZ110	S111 F/F 22/03/76 (A. Love) and originally incorrectly assigned serial XY110. D/D to RAF Laarbruch 05/04/76 for II (AC) Squadron as 'J'. Re-coded '30' by 08/80 but lost in a crash on 16/06/83 at CFB Goose Bay, following a collision with XZ105.
XZ111	S112 F/F 22/03/76 (E. Bucklow) and originally incorrectly assigned serial XY111. D/D to RAF Laarbruch 07/04/76 for II (AC) Squadron as code 'A'. Re-coded '31' by 08/80, it was transferred to 6 Squadron on 27/01/89 as 'EL'. Received desert pink ARTF scheme in 12/92 and had gained the inscription 'Thunderbird 1' on nose. Re-assigned to 54 Squadron as 'GO' it was dispatched to RAF Shawbury for a period of short-term store on 07/09/93, until given an overhaul at St Athan in 10/95. Repainted in new grey colour scheme in 07/96. Returned to 54 Squadron as 'GO' but was lost in a crash on 27/10/00, some 5 miles north-east of Dumfries, following a bird strike.

With a Vinton Vicon 18 Series 601 EO GP (1) pod on the centre-line, XZ104 'FM' of No.41 (F) Squadron, had been upgraded to GR.3A by the time this photograph was taken in May 2003.

Flown by Fl. Lt Graham Wright XZ107, sporting an Arctic camouflage scheme, takes on fuel from a No.101 Squadron VC.10K2.

Probably the most photographed RAF Jaguar, XZ112, seen here at RIAT 05 sporting the special RAF Coltishall '65th Anniversary' scheme, has worn no less than three commemorative schemes.

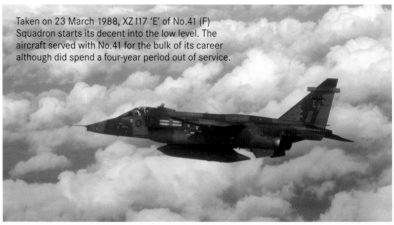

Taken on 23 March 1988, XZ117 'E' of No.41 (F) Squadron starts its decent into the low level. The aircraft served with No.41 for the bulk of its career although did spend a four-year period out of service.

XZ112	S113 F/F 22/03/76 (A. Love) and originally incorrectly assigned serial XY112. D/D to RAF Laarbruch 12/04/76 for II (AC) Squadron as code 'G'. Re-coded '32', it was upgraded to GR.1A at JMU in 11/82 and flown to RAF Shawbury for short-term store in 01/89. Following overhaul by JMU and 'stage three' modifications it was delivered to RAF Coltishall in 02/91 and received '75th Anniversary' markings for No.54 Squadron. Assigned code 'GA', it received the grey ARTF scheme in 06/93 and again in 09/94 for UN peacekeeping operations. Repainted in new grey colour scheme in 12/95, it was upgraded to GR.3 at St Athan in 10/99 and GR.3A in 06/01. Received 54 Squadron '89th Anniversary' markings in 01/05 and, in the post-disbandment re-shuffle, was assigned to 41 Squadron as 'FE'. Received, on 29/06/05, a special RAF Coltishall '65th Anniversary' scheme instead. Although nominally on 41 Squadron strength, it sports the code 'GW' on the nwd. Flown to RAF Shawbury for store 12/04/06.
XZ113	S114 F/F 02/04/76 (A. Love) and originally incorrectly assigned serial XY113. D/D to RAF Coltishall 27/04/76 for 41 Squadron code 'A'. It was the first aircraft in 01/83 to received modified squadron markings of white outlined sidebars and red/white/red fin band passing through the white outlined code. Loaned to II (AC) Squadron as '30' by 08/83 and upgraded to GR.1A on 20/02/85. Transferred to 54 Squadron as 'GA' by 01/89 and back to 41 Squadron as 'D' in 08/89. Received desert pink ARTF scheme as a spare aircraft for Operation Granby with the code 'FD'. It undertook a number of UN peacekeeping operations in 1993 sporting the grey ARTF scheme and had by this time received the 'stage three' modifications. Painted in desert pink ARTF for Exercise Jagged Sphinx in 12/96 it was upgraded to GR.3 in mid-1998 and GR.3A in 03/03. Loaned to SAOEU in 08/03, it was on 41 Squadron strength as 'FD' until 03/06, when flown to St Athan.
XZ114	S115 F/F 08/04/76 (E. Bucklow) and originally incorrectly assigned serial XY114. D/D to RAF Coltishall 06/05/76 for 41 Squadron as code 'B'. Received an Arctic ARTF scheme for deployment to Bardufoss in 02/86, desert pink ARTF with code 'FB' in 03/93, and ARTF grey in 06/93, but returned to normal camouflage as 'B' in 01/94, only to receive the ARTF desert pink scheme again in 06/94. Dispatched to RAF Shawbury for storage on 12/12/94, it remained at that location until transported by road to St Athan on 10/04/03 for overhaul and upgrading to GR.3A standard. Re-issued to 41 Squadron as 'FB' on 05/05/04 but, in the post-disbandment re-shuffle, was assigned to 6 Squadron as 'EO'. Flown to RAF Shawbury for storage 11/04/06.
XZ115	S116 F/F 30/04/76 (E. Bucklow) and originally incorrectly assigned serial XY115. D/D to RAF Coltishall 04/06/76 for 41 Squadron, code 'C'. Upgraded to GR.1A at JMU in 06/86, it was loaned to II (AC) Squadron as '23' on 23/08/88 but was back with 41 Squadron again as 'C' on 26/01/89. Received an Arctic camouflage scheme for a deployment to Bardufoss in 02/90 and then painted in desert pink ARTF for Operation Granby and coded 'FC'. Dispatched to RAF Shawbury for short-term storage in 08/94 then by road to St Athan via Coltishall on 05/12/95. Overhauled and repainted in new grey scheme it returned to 41 Squadron as 'FC', having been re-designated GR.1B(R). Loaned to SAOEU in 01/97, it was transferred to 16 (Reserve) Squadron by 12/01 as 'PD', by which time it was designated a GR.3. Upgraded again to GR.3A at St Athan in 12/04 in the post-disbandment re-shuffle, it was assigned to 6 Squadron as 'ER'.
XZ116	S117 F/F 22/04/76 (P. Ginger) and originally incorrectly assigned serial XY116. D/D to RAF Coltishall 28/05/76 for 41 Squadron, code 'D'. Received an experimental blue/white ARTF camouflage scheme for Exercise Teamwork at Bardufoss in 03/84. Upgraded to GR.1A at the JMU in 11/86 but was lost in a crash on 17/06/87 when it collided with Tornado GR.1 ZA493 'GH' of 20 Squadron head-on in Barrowdale Valley, Cumbria, with the loss of the pilot. This accident led to the introduction of flow routes in the low-flying areas.
XZ117	S118 F/F 29/04/76 (A. Love) and originally incorrectly assigned serial XY117. D/D to RAF Coltishall 28/05/76 for 41 Squadron, code 'E'. Upgraded to GR.1A at JMU in 01/87 and later re-coded 'P' in late 1990. Transferred to 54 Squadron as 'GG' in 04/91, it received a desert pink ARTF scheme for Operation Warden in late 1992 and Arctic camouflage in 06/94. Flown to RAF Shawbury for short-term store on 12/07/94 it was removed by road to RAF Coltishall on 05/12/95 and then on to St Athan on 10/07/96 for overhaul and upgrade to GR.3 standard. Re-issued to 6 Squadron as 'EP' it was back at St Athan on 10/07/01 for upgrading to GR.3A and the Adour 106 re-engining. F/F in this configuration in 06/02 and then returned to 6 Squadron. Received an ARTF scheme in 02/03 for the second Iraq War but not deployed and returned to the standard new grey scheme by 07/03. In the post-disbandment re-shuffle, allocated to 41 Squadron as 'FB'.
XZ118	S119 F/F 12/05/76 (D. Eagles) and originally incorrectly assigned serial XY118. D/D to RAF Coltishall 24/05/76 for 41 Squadron as 'F'. Upgraded to GR.1A at JMU in 10/86, it was to receive Gulf War modifications and the ARTF desert pink scheme, being deployed to Thumrait on 02/11/90. Named 'Buster Gonad' with the code 'Y' on nwd, it returned to the UK on 13/03/91, sporting thirty-eight mission symbols. Retaining ARTF scheme, but coded 'FF', it was one of the first eight jets to deploy to Incirlik under Operation Warden on 04/09/91. Having received the 'stage three' modifications, it was used extensively on UN peacekeeping operations, receiving new grey scheme in 06/93 and 07/96 with the application of the new permanent grey scheme in 01/97. Upgraded to GR.3 at St Athan in late 1998 and GR.3A in 04/04, it was assigned the code 'FR' in the post-disbandment re-shuffle. Wfu St Athan by 03/06.
XZ119	S120 F/F 18/05/76 (P. Ginger) and originally incorrectly assigned serial XY119. D/D to RAF Coltishall 28/05/76 for 41 Squadron code 'G'. Loaned to ETPS in 01/82, it was to receive Gulf War modifications and desert pink ARTF scheme, deploying to Thumrait on 23/10/90. Given the nose art 'Katrina Jane' and the code 'Z' on the nwd, it returned to the UK on 12/03/91 with forty mission symbols, returning to 41 Squadron as 'FG'. One of the first eight aircraft to deploy to Incirlik as part of Operation Warden on 04/09/91. Despite later returning to normal camouflage, it retained its nose art and mission symbols until at least 03/93. Wfu and stored at RAF Coltishall pending disposal in 06/96, it was taken by road to RAF Cranwell for ground instructional duties as 9266M, where it remains today.

One of No.41 (F) Squadron's original mounts, XZ356 is seen here in desert pink and sporting the 'Mary Rose' nose art and Operation Granby mission marks. The jet is equipped with AIM−9L Sidewinder missiles on the over-wing rails, two 1,000lb bombs on each inner wing station and an AN/ALE−101 ECM pod on the port outer station. It probably carried a 'Phimat' chaff/flare dispenser on the starboard outer.

XZ120	S121 F/F 19/05/76 (P. Ginger) and originally incorrectly assigned serial XY120. D/D to RAF Laarbruch 15/06/76 for II (AC) Squadron as code '20', it was lost in a crash off Nordholm, Denmark, on 25/02/77. Wreck recovered and disposed of to Park Aviation Supply, Faygate, Sussex.
XZ355	S122 F/F 10/06/76 (E. Bucklow) and D/D RAF Coltishall 08/07/76 for 41 Squadron, code 'H'. Transferred to 54 Squadron as 'GA' 14/04/82 but back to 41 Squadron as 'J' 09/03/84. Upgraded to GR.1A at JMU in 08/86 and noted sporting a striped Arctic camouflage for deployment to Bardufoss in 02/90. Received desert pink ARTF scheme in 08/90 for Operation Granby and coded 'FJ' in 01/91. Deployed to Incirlik on Operation Warden duties on 04/09/91, having received the 'stage three' modifications. Returned to 41 Squadron 'J' by 02/95, only to receive Arctic camouflage for Exercise Strong Resolve the same month. Loaned to Boscombe Down in 07/96 as a GR.1A and received the new grey camouflage scheme at St Athan on 07/10/97. Upgraded to GR.3 in 10/98 and GR.3A in 08/01, it was on 41 Squadron strength as code 'FJ' until wfu St Athan by 04/06.

XZ356	S123 F/F 07/06/76 (E. Bucklow) and D/D to RAF Coltishall 09/07/76 for 41 Squadron as code 'J'. Incurred a bird strike and placed in short-term store at the JMU by 09/78. Repaired and re-issued to 17 Squadron as 'BP' on 27/10/80. Re-coded 'BJ' by 04/84 and then transferred to 14 Squadron as 'AU' by 04/85. To JMU for upgrade to GR.1A and issued to 41 Squadron again as 'J' 24/02/86. Re-coded 'R' post-overhaul in 08/90, and painted in desert pink ARTF camouflage as spare aircraft for Operation Granby. Upgraded with Gulf War modifications, it was deployed to Thumrait on 02/11/90, where it received 'Mary Rose' nose art and the code 'N' on the nwd. It returned to the UK 12/03/91 with thirty-three mission symbols. Re-assigned to 6 Squadron as 'EP' it had lost its desert pink scheme by 10/92 only to have it re-applied the following month. Repainted in ARTF grey by 06/93 for UN peacekeeping operations, it was dispatched to St Athan in 08/97 only to be re-directed to RAF Shawbury for storage, where it remained until 09/03/01, when it was taken back to St Athan by road for overhaul and upgrade. Issued to 54 Squadron on 30/05/02 as a GR.3A and coded 'GF', but immediately loaned to SAOEU for a month. Re-assigned to 41 Squadron and allocated code 'FU' in post-disbandment re-shuffle. Wfu St Athan by 03/06.

XZ357	S124 F/F 17/06/76 (A. Love) and D/D to RAF Coltishall 16/07/76 for 41 Squadron as code 'K'. Underwent engine upgrade by 06/78, becoming the first aircraft to receive Dash-26 engines. Later received light blue/grey Arctic scheme for Exercise Alloy Express in early 1982. To JMU on 02/01/86 for GR.1A upgrade and overhaul, returning to the unit as 'K'. Received the desert pink ARTF scheme for Operation Granby but did not participate in hostilities, and had returned to standard camouflage by 04/91. Received ARTF grey for UN peacekeeping operations in 07/93, then, while on overhaul at St Athan, became the first Jaguar to receive the new permanent grey scheme in 02/95. Upgraded to Jaguar 96 in 02/99 with 41 Squadron as 'FK', then GR.3A at St Athan in 09/01. Was wfu by 10/04 and fuselage minus cockpit section dispatched to St Athan for spares reclamation on 28/10/04.
XZ358	S125 F/F 25/06/76 (E. Bucklow) and fitted with Dash-26 engines for demonstation at 1976 SBAC show. D/D to RAF Coltishall 02/11/76 for 41 Squadron as code 'L'. Suffered a ground fire 21/02/77 but was repaired. Noted sporting the light blue/grey Arctic camouflage for Exercise Alloy Express in early 1982. Received similar treatment in 03/85 for another deployment to Norway before upgrading to GR.1A. In 1990 received Gulf War modifications and the desert pink ARTF colour scheme. Deployed to Thumrait on 23/10/90 where it received the nose art 'Diplomatic Service' and the code 'W' on the nwd. It returned to the UK 13/03/91 with four mission symbols. Coded 'FL' it retained its desert scheme and deployed to Incirlik on 04/09/91 under Operation Warden. It remained with the squadron, receiving ARTF schemes in support of UN peacekeeping operations until wfu at RAF Coltishall in 07/96. Re-assigned to ground instructional duties, it was dispatched to RAF Cranwell on 15/10/96 for use by the Aircraft Maintenance Instruction Flight as 9262M, where it remains in use today.
XZ359	S126 F/F 08/07/76 (E. Bucklow) and D/D to RAF Coltishall 25/08/76 for 41 Squadron as code 'M'. Received the light blue/grey Arctic scheme for Exercise Alloy Express in 1982, and was upgraded to GR.1A at the JMU in 07/86. Once again it deployed to Bardufoss sporting an Arctic scheme in 01/89, but was lost in a crash on 13/04/89 when it struck cliffs at St Abbs Head, Berwick, killing the pilot.
XZ360	S127 F/F 14/09/76 (R. Stock) and D/D to RAF Abingdon 31/08/76 for storage. Issued to 41 Squadron 29/04/77 as 'Y', it was re-coded 'N' on 08/02/84 and upgraded to GR.1A at the JMU in 07/86. Received 'stage three' modifications and participated in overseas UN peacekeeping operations, receiving an ARTF grey scheme and the code 'FN', in 09/94, 08/95, 01/97. Upgraded to Jaguar 96 at St Athan in 09/98 and re-designated GR.3 in 09/00. GR.3A modifications came in 02/03 and the jet was painted in ARTF again for second Iraq War but never deployed. Wfu St Athan by 03/06.

A near perfect portrait shot of Jaguar GR.1A XZ361 'FT' of No.41 (F) Squadron taken on 13 October 1998. The photograph was shot on Fuji Velvia 50 using a Nikon F90X with a 2.8D 80–200mm zoom lens.

XZ361	S128 F/F 04/08/76 (R. Stock) and D/D to RAF Abingdon 02/09/76 for storage. Issued to II (AC) Squadron as 'II' on 16/03/77 it was re-coded '20' by 08/80 and '25' by 07/83. Upgraded to GR.1A at the JMU in 02/85, it was returned to the unit but then flown to RAF Shawbury by 01/89 for short-term storage. Overhauled at St Athan in 09/92, it was issued to 41 Squadron, taking the code 'T'. Received an Arctic scheme for Exercise Battle Griffin in 02/95 and again in 03/96. Re-coded 'FT', it was upgraded to GR.3 at St Athan in 2000 but flown to RAF Shawbury again on 26/06/02 for storage, where it has remained until put up for disposal by tender DSAT 3146 on 26/05/05. Sold to D. Everett Aero, Sproughton, Suffolk. Departed for its new home on 15/12/05. Now displayed at the former USAFE base at Bentwaters.
XZ362	S129 F/F 19/08/76 (A. Love) and displayed at 1976 SBAC show. D/D 27/09/76 to RAF Abingdon prior to delivery to II (AC) Squadron. Taking the code '19' by 08/80 and then '27' by 01/82, it was transferred to 41 Squadron as code 'E' 25/05/90 followed by 54 Squadron as 'GC' in 04/93. Received ARTF grey scheme for UN peacekeeping duties in 06/93 and again in 09/94. It received the 'stage three' modifications and became the first 54 Squadron aircraft to receive the new permanent grey scheme on 23/01/96. It was lost in a crash on 24/07/96 during DACT (Dissimilar Air Combat Training) while participating in Exercise Cope Thunder in Alaska. The 41 Squadron pilot ejected safely.
XZ363	S130 F/F 25/08/76 (J.J. Cockburn) and D/D to RAF Abingdon 14/09/76 for storage. Issued to 41 Squadron by 08/77 as code 'Z', it was re-coded 'A' by 09/83 and upgraded to GR.1A at the JMU in 10/86. Painted in a special anniversary colour scheme in 10/90 of red fin containing white flash with cross of Lorraine at the top. Later, in 08/90, received the desert pink ARTF scheme for Operation Granby, but did not participate in hostilities. Coded 'FA' by 01/91 and then 'FO' in 06/91, it had retained its ARTF finish before returning to normal camouflage by 10/92. Desert pink applied once again in 11/92 for a period of UN peacekeeping duties, but in 05/93 received a white and green Arctic scheme. Flown to RAF Shawbury by 10/95 for a period of short-term store, then to St Athan for overhaul, emerging on 13/11/96 as a GR.1B(R) and in the new grey colour scheme. Then loaned to Boscombe Down. Returned to 41 Squadron as 'FO' as a GR.3 but lost in a crash on 25/07/01 while being flown by a 54 Squadron pilot during Exercise Cope Thunder.

Jaguar GR.1 XZ358 'L' of No.41 (F) Squadron landing at RAF Coltishall on 26 April 1983.

XZ364 '21' of No.II (AC) Squadron outside its
shelter complex at RAF Laarbruch.

Not quite sure what the pilot is holding towards the camera, but the jet XZ366 'FC' of No.41 (F) Squadron was upgraded to Jaguar GR.3A in late 2000 having only served with the two dedicated Jaguar reconnaissance squadrons.

XZ364	S131 F/F 03/09/76 (R.J. Stock) and D/D to RAF Abingdon 27/09/76 for storage. Issued to II (AC) Squadron by 08/80 as '18' but re-coded '21' by 01/83. Upgraded to GR.1A at JMU in 02/85 and transferred to 54 Squadron as 'GJ' in 01/89. Received Gulf War modifications and the desert pink colour scheme and deployed to Thumrait on 23/10/90. Here it received the 'Sadman' nose art and the code 'Q' on the nwd. Returned to UK 01/03/91 with forty-seven mission marks, and repainted in standard camouflage by 06/91. ARTF grey applied in 06/93 and again in 09/94. In 1996, after a period of loan to Boscombe Down and overhaul at St Athan, the jet was repainted in the new grey colour scheme. Reported as both a GR.1B(R) and GR.1B(T), it was upgraded to GR.3 at St Athan in 05/99 and later to GR.3A. Received special RAF Coltishall '60th Anniversary' markings on 29/06/00 and, following the disbandment of 54 Squadron, was re-assigned to 41 Squadron as 'FS' in the resulting re-shuffle, but wfu St Athan by 03/06.
XZ365	S132 F/F 19/09/76 (E. Bucklow) and D/D to RAF Abingdon 01/10/76 for storage. Issued to 41 Squadron as 'D' by 09/77 but re-coded 'J' by 06/79, and became the first squadron aircraft to receive modified unit insignia with previous red markings outlined in white. Became the third aircraft to receive the avionics update to GR.1A standard and the second to be outshopped by the JMU on 09/03/84. Re-assigned to 54 Squadron as 'GC' on 14/03/84 and then to II (AC) Squadron as '33' in 08/84. It was then lost in a crash near Meschede, east of Dortmund, West Germany, on 09/07/85.
XZ366	S133 F/F 20/09/76 (R. Stock) and D/D to RAF Abingdon 06/10/76 for storage. Issued to II (AC) Squadron in 1978 and coded '22' by 09/80 it was upgraded at the JMU in 07/84 to GR.1A standard. Following conversion by II (AC) Squadron to Tornado GR.1A the jet was flown to RAF Shawbury for storage in 01/89, remaining there until at least 06/92. Re-issued to 41 Squadron as 'S' on 04/06/92 it was involved in visibility trials flying with white external tanks. Received an Arctic scheme in 02/95 when participating in Exercise Strong Resolve, and it emerged from St Athan on 24/07/95 sporting the new permanent grey colour scheme, having been upgraded to GR.1A. Re-coded 'FS', the jet was modified to Jaguar 96 configuration at St Athan in 03/99, then GR.3A in 12/00. In the resulting re-shuffle following the disbandment of 16 and 54 Squadrons, was allocated the code 'FC'. Flown to St Athan and allocated to DCAE Cosford in 03/06.
XZ367	S134 F/F 06/10/76 (E. Bucklow) and D/D to RAF Abingdon 01/11/76 for storage. Issued to II (AC) Squadron as 'H' by 05/77 but returned to store at JMU in 01/78, where it remained until at least 06/80. Re-issued to 226 OCU as '25' on 30/06/81, it was upgraded to GR.1A on 31/10/85 and returned to II (AC) Squadron as '33' before being re-coded '20'. Transferred to 54 Squadron as 'GP' on 18/01/89, it was to receive the Gulf War modifications and desert pink colour scheme, being deployed to Thumrait on 23/10/90. Here it received the nose art 'Debbie', but later changed to 'White Rose', and the code 'P' on the nwd. Returned to UK 13/03/91 sporting forty mission symbols and

	had returned to standard camouflage by 05/91. Dispatched to JMU 14/06/91 for overhaul, becoming last of type to be overhauled at Abingdon. Returned to 54 Squadron by 01/92, and it received 'stage three' modifications at St Athan in 07/94 as well as a grey ARTF scheme in 02/95 for UN peacekeeping operations. Returned to desert pink in 11/96 for Exercise Desert Sphinx and, upon return, placed in short-term store at RAF Coltishall. Upgraded to GR.3A at St Athan in 03/00 but overstressed during Operation Warden at Incirlik. Returned to Coltishall and then taken by road to RAF Shawbury for storage on 29/09/00, where it remained until returning to Coltishall on 02/10/02 in the ground instructional role as a weapon loading training airframe. While in this role it received the 6 Squadron anniversary scheme fin prior to its application on XX112.
XZ368	S135 F/F 01/10/76 (E. Bucklow) and D/D to RAF Bruggen 01/11/76 for 14 Squadron as code 'AN'. Re-assigned to 6 Squadron on 11/06/79, becoming code 'EL'. Returned to 14 Squadron on 07/02/84 as 'AG', before returning to Coltishall in 10/85. Assigned to ground instructional duties at Cosford on 27/10/86, it was to receive the maintenance serial 8900M, and it remains here in that role today.
XZ369	S136 F/F 11/10/76 (J.J. Lee) and D/D to RAF Bruggen 01/11/76 for 14 Squadron as 'AP'. Transferred to 17 Squadron as 'BF' by 10/83, then sent to RAF Shawbury on 05/03/85 for short-term storage. Upgraded to GR.1A and issued to 6 Squadron as 'EE' on 03/03/87 but re-coded 'EF' following overhaul at JMU in 05/89. Received the desert pink ARTF scheme for Operation Granby, but did not take part in hostilities. Used on UN peacekeeping operations post-Granby, receiving the grey ARTF finish in 06/93 and 09/94. Upgraded to GR.1B at St Athan in 10/95 and immediately undertook overseas operations, again sporting the grey ARTF finish. With St Athan on overhaul 21/10/96 through to 21/08/97 it was returned to 6 Squadron as a Jaguar 96(T), then, in 09/00, upgraded to GR.3A at St Athan. Assigned to 6 Squadron but allocated the code 'EU' in the post-disbandment re-shuffle. Flown to St Athan and assigned to DCAE Cosford by 03/06.
XZ370	S137 F/F 20/10/76 (E. Bucklow) and D/D to RAF Bruggen 04/11/76 for 14 Squadron but passed to 17 Squadron as 'BN'. Returned to UK on 20/03/85 into storage at RAF Shawbury and assigned to ground instructional training at RAF Cosford. Allocated maintenance serial 9004M and coded 'JB', it had arrived at Cosford by 01/00, where it remains today.
XZ371	S138 F/F 03/11/76 (E. Bucklow) and D/D to RAF Bruggen 07/12/76 for 17 Squadron as 'BP'. During a NATO exchange with JaBoG.32, received a JaBoG.32 badge beneath the cockpit, with the serial 17+32 and the inscription 'Lechfeld Airlines'. Re-coded 'BB' before transfer to 14 Squadron as 'AP' by 08/84. Flown to RAF Shawbury 13/12/85 for storage and assigned to ground instructional training at RAF Cosford, where it still resides today. Allocated maintenance serial 8907M, it had arrived by 01/00.

A 'batch two' aircraft issued to No.14 Squadron factory fresh on 1 November 1976. XZ369 'AP' is seen here on approach to RAF Coningsby on 25 March 1982.

The Coltishall weapon load trainer, XZ367, wearing the No.6 Squadron '90th Anniversary' markings.

XZ372	S139 F/F 10/11/76 (E. Bucklow) and D/D to RAF Bruggen 07/12/76 for 14 Squadron, code 'AQ'. Transferred to 20 Squadron as 'CB' by 10/83 then re-assigned to 226 OCU as '04' on 18/01/84. Upgraded to GR.1A at JMU in 09/85, it was re-issued to 6 Squadron as 'ED'. Painted in desert pink ARTF for Operation Granby, the jet did not participate in hostilities, but, by 02/95, had received the 'stage three' modifications. Noted sporting Arctic camouflage in 02/95 for participation in Exercise Strong Resolve and later, in 09/96, noted in store at Boscombe Down. Dispatched to St Athan for further storage, it remained here until 07/02/00, when it entered the overhaul and upgrade programme. Re-issued to 6 Squadron coded 'ED' on 30/11/00 as a GR.3A, it was transferred to 41 Squadron as 'FV' in the post-disbandment re-shuffle, but has subsequently been wfu at St Athan, where it arrived on 05/07/05.
XZ373	S140 F/F 19/11/76 (R. Stock) and D/D to RAF Bruggen 07/12/76 for 17 Squadron as 'BQ'. Re-coded 'BB' when dispatched to JMU for overhaul in 04/81, it was later transferred to 20 Squadron as 'CG' by 11/83. Flown to RAF Shawbury for short-term store on 14/07/84, it was returned to JMU in 09/84 for upgrade to GR.1A and was delivered to 6 Squadron as 'EC' on 28/01/85. Re-assigned to 54 Squadron as 'GF' y 06/88 it was to receive the 'stage three' modifications to permit overseas peacekeeping duties and was noted sporting the grey ARTF in 09/93. Still with 54 Squadron, it was lost during an ACM sortie over the Adriatic on 26/06/95, with the USAF exchange pilot ejecting safely.
XZ374	S141 F/F 09/12/76 (E. Bucklow) and D/D to RAF Bruggen 05/01/77 for 20 Squadron, code 'CA'. Transferred to 14 Squadron as 'AD' by 10/83, then flown to RAF Shawbury on 13/08/85 for storage, but allocated to ground instructional duties as 9005M at RAF Cosford. Coded 'JC' with the school, it is still in use today.
XZ375	S142 F/F 16/12/76 (E. Bucklow) and D/D to RAF Bruggen 24/01/77 for 20 Squadron as 'CB'. Re-assigned to 14 Squadron as 'AK' by 10/83. It was upgraded at JMU to GR.1A standard in 02/86, and transferred to 54 Squadron as 'GB'. Stored at JMU between 21/09/87 and 23/10/90, by which time it had received Gulf War modifications and the desert pink ARTF colour scheme. Flown to Thumrait 23/10/90, it was to receive the nose art 'Guardian Reader' and the code 'S' on the nwd. Returned to the UK 12/03/91 sporting seventeen mission symbols and returned to 54 Squadron as 'GR'. It retained its desert pink ARTF scheme and deployed again on 09/09/91 to Incirlik on Operation Warden. Later received the ARTF grey scheme for future UN peacekeeping operations, and the 'stage three' modifications. Overhauled at St Athan in 08/95, emerging in the new grey scheme and updated to GR.1B standard. However, it was placed in store and allocated to ground instructional duties as 9255M with the DARA civilian technical training school, where it was noted in 01/97. Wfu and dispatched by road to RAF Coltishall on 19/02/02 when the forward fuselage section was acquired by Mick Jennings for his cockpit collection. This was repainted in desert pink and the 'Guardian Reader' inscription put back on. The remainder was used for BDRT.
XZ376	S143 F/F 13/01/77 (R. Stock) and D/D to RAF Bruggen for 14 Squadron as 'AE'. Transferred to 17 Squadron as 'BE' by 09/78 but lost in a crash on Tain range, Scotland, on 07/03/83, with the pilot ejecting safely.
XZ377	S144 F/F 21/01/77 (A. Love) and D/D to RAF Bruggen 15/02/77 for 20 Squadron as code 'CF'. Transferred to 31 Squadron as 'DF' by 03/84, and II (AC) Squadron in 11/84 as code '39'. To JMU 06/02/85 for overhaul and upgrade to GR.1A, before re-issue to 226 OCU, code '02'. Transferred to 54 Squadron 11/02/87 and on to 6 Squadron as 'EB', when it received the desert pink ARTF scheme as a spare aircraft for Operation Granby. Passed to 16 (Reserve) Squadron as 'B' in 04/97, then to St Athan for upgrade to Jaguar 96 configuration, upon which it returned to 6 Squadron as 'EG'. Noted sporting the ARTF grey scheme in 01/03 for second Iraq War, but not deployed. Upgraded again at St Athan between 02/04/04 and 19/01/05 to GR.3A, and allocated code 'EP' in the post-disbandment re-shuffle. Wfu St Athan by 04/06.
XZ378	S145 F/F 01/02/77 (E. Bucklow) and D/D to RAF Bruggen 15/02/77 for 20 Squadron as code 'CH'. Transferred to 31 Squadron as 'DG' by 12/83, to 17 Squadron as 'BB' by 06/84, and finally to 41 Squadron as 'P', before dispatch to JMU for upgrade to GR.1A in 07/85. Re-issued to 6 Squadron as 'EP', it was flown to RAF Shawbury 10/90 for storage, where it has remained, but was put up for disposal on 26/05/05 under DSAT 3146. Sold 14/11/05 to a Mr Langdon.

With a CBLS on the centre-line station and two external tanks Jaguar GR.1 XZ378 'BB', No.17 Squadron, taxis out at RAF Waddington on 10 October 1984.

XZ381	S146 F/F 16/02/77 (E. Bucklow) and D/D 17/03/77 to RAF Bruggen for 20 Squadron, code 'CD'. Transferred to 17 Squadron, code 'BL', by 01/84, before being flown to RAF Shawbury on 20/03/85 for storage. Taken to JMU for overhaul in 03/89 and re-issued to 54 Squadron as 'GB'. Painted in desert pink ARTF and deployed to Incirlik on 09/09/91 as part of Operation Warden, having received the 'stage three' modifications. Transferred to 6 Squadron as 'EC' by 03/93 and noted wearing the ARTF grey scheme in 06/93. To JMU again on 28/06/94, followed by a period at Boscombe Down for TIALD integration, returning to Coltishall by 01/96, designated as GR.1B. Dispatched to St Athan 26/07/96 for modification and painting in the new grey scheme, then again in 10/08/98 to be brought up to Jaguar 96 standard. Transferred to 16 (Reserve) Squadron and allocated the code 'D', it gained an all black fin with a yellow saint marking but was lost in a crash on 20/10/99, 6 miles north of RAF Lossiemouth in the Moray Firth. Pilot ejected safely.
XZ382	S147 F/F 10/03/77 (E. Bucklow) and D/D to RAF Bruggen 06/04/77 for 17 Squadron as 'BE'. Transferred to 14 Squadron as 'AE' by 09/78, it was flown to the JMU in 03/80 where it remained until at least 11/82. It was moved to St Athan by 05/83 and RAF Shawbury by 11/85 at which point it was assigned to the ground instructional role. Allocated maintenance serial 8908M, it was dispatched to No.1 SoTT at RAF Halton by 12/86. Following the closure of the unit was taken to RAF Coltishall on 13/10/92 for BDRT, where it remained until at least 05/98, but has subsequently been passed into the hands of the preservationists at Bruntingthorpe.
XZ383	S148 F/F 11/03/77 (A. Love) and D/D to RAF Bruggen on 19/04/77 for 17 Squadron, code 'BC'. Transferred to 14 Squadron as 'AF' by 11/83, it was flown to RAF Coltishall in 10/85 before being relegated to the ground instructional role. Dispatched to RAF Cosford on 27/10/86 with maintenance serial 8901M, it remains in use today.
XZ384	S149 F/F 18/03/77 (E. Bucklow) and D/D to RAF Bruggen 06/04/77 for 20 Squadron as 'CM'. Re-assigned to 31 Squadron as 'DG' on 10/07/84 but passed to 17 Squadron as 'BC' in 10/84. Flown to RAF Shawbury for storage on 28/02/85 before being assigned to ground instructional duties at No.2 SoTT RAF Cosford in 03/88. Assigned the maintenance serial 8954M, it remains in use today.

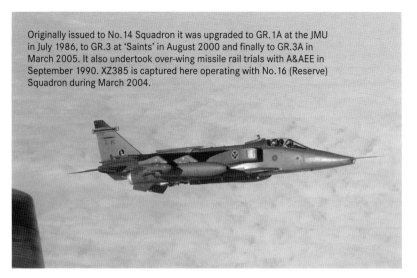

Originally issued to No.14 Squadron it was upgraded to GR.1A at the JMU in July 1986, to GR.3 at 'Saints' in August 2000 and finally to GR.3A in March 2005. It also undertook over-wing missile rail trials with A&AEE in September 1990. XZ385 is captured here operating with No.16 (Reserve) Squadron during March 2004.

Jaguar GR.1 XZ390 'DN' of No.31 Squadron captured landing at RAF Coningsby on 25 March 1982.

XZ385	S150 F/F 25/03/77 (E. Bucklow) and D/D RAF Bruggen 21/04/77 for 14 Squadron as 'AG'. Re-coded 'AA' in 10/82, it was transferred to 17 Squadron as 'BE' by 06/83 prior to dispatch to the JMU in early 1985. Re-issued to 41 Squadron in 04/85 but assigned to the 'Gib Det' as 'G' prior to joining 6 Squadron as 'EK' by 09/85. Upgraded at JMU to GR.1A in 07/86. Joined 54 Squadron as 'GM' but was loaned to Boscombe Down in 09/90 for fitment and trials with over-wing missile rails. Transferred to 16 (Reserve) Squadron as '03' by 09/93 following overhaul at St Athan. Re-coded 'F' in 03/94 before receiving the new grey colour scheme and the code 'C'. Loaned to 6 Squadron following upgrade to GR.1A, returning to 16 (Reserve) Squadron as 'R' and then sent to St Athan for overhaul and modification to GR.3. The jet returned to 16 (Reserve) Squadron as 'C' in 08/00 but was upgraded to GR.3A at St Athan in 12/03 and re-coded 'PC'. Assigned to 41 Squadron as 'FT' in the post-disbandment re-shuffle. Wfu St Athan by 03/06.
XZ386	S151 F/F 19/04/77 (E. Bucklow) and D/D to RAF Bruggen, via RAF Coltishall, 16/05/77 for 14 Squadron as 'AJ'. Transferred to 31 Squadron as 'DB' by 12/83 but flown to UK on 24/10/84 following unit's transition to Tornado. Re-issued to II (AC) Squadron as '38' but re-coded '32' in 04/85. Became part of 'Gib Det' as 'B' then re-assigned to 6 Squadron as 'EK' by 10/85. Upgraded to GR.1A at JMU in 12/85 and re-assigned to 226 OCU as '05' in 02/86 but crashed on 24/06/87 into a hillside near Aberedu, Powys, Wales, with the loss of the pilot.
XZ387	S152 F/F 06/05/77 (E. Bucklow) and D/D to RAF Bruggen 26/05/77 for 31 Squadron where it took the code 'DN'. Returned to the UK on 02/11/84. It was upgraded at the JMU to GR.1A and re-issued to 6 Squadron as 'EB' before transfer to 54 Squadron as 'GG' in 03/90. Crashed on 12/09/90 into the Solway Firth, 5 miles off Southerness Point, Dumfries & Galloway, with the loss of the pilot. Rear section and wing recovered by the diving vessel Oliver Felix in 09/93.
XZ388	S153 F/F 12/05/77 (E. Bucklow) and D/D to RAF Bruggen on 05/06/77 for 17 Squadron as 'BK'. Transferred to 14 Squadron as 'AH' but lost in a crash near Rebberlah, north-east of Celle, West Germany, on 02/04/85, with the pilot ejecting safely.
XZ389	S154 F/F 07/05/77 (R. Stock) and D/D to RAF Bruggen 24/06/77 for 20 Squadron as 'CN'. Transferred to 31 Squadron in 10/83 as 'DM' and then to 17 Squadron as 'BL' in 10/84, the jet was flown to RAF Shawbury on 28/02/85 for storage. Allocated to ground instructional duties at RAF Halton, it had arrived with No.1 SoTT by 03/88 and assigned maintenance serial 8946M. At closure of unit, transferred to RAF Cosford, where it still resides today.

XZ390	S155 F/F 09/06/77 (J.J. Lee) and D/D to RAF Bruggen 05/07/77 for 31 Squadron as 'DM'. Following overhaul at JMU it was re-assigned to 20 Squadron as 'CL', then transferred to II (AC) Squadron as '35' by 07/84. Flown to RAF Shawbury on 25/04/85 for storage, it was later assigned to ground instructional duties at No.2 SoTT RAF Cosford, with maintenance serial 9003M, where it remains today.
XZ391	S156 F/F 23/06/77 (J.J. Lee) and D/D to RAF Bruggen 15/07/77 for 31 Squadron as 'DP'. Re-coded 'DF' on 15/09/82, it was dispatched to JMU in 02/84 for overhaul and upgrading to GR.1A, following which it was re-issued to 54 Squadron as 'GE' on 21/06/84. Re-coded 'GN' after attention at the JMU in 04/87, it was flown to RAF Shawbury for storage on 12/02/90 but had departed for overhaul at St Athan by 02/91, and was issued to 226 OCU as '05' on 21/11/91. Returned to 54 Squadron as 'GM' by 06/92. Had ARTF grey applied for UN peacekeeping operations in 06/93 and undertook the high-visibility trials with white external tanks in 02/95. Overhaul again at St Athan saw the jet emerge on 01/03/96 in the new grey colour scheme, and it was transferred to 16 (Reserve) Squadron as 'A' on 30/07/96. A return to St Athan beckoned in 02/99 when it was modified to Jaguar 96 standard. On 28/05/99, it was re-assigned to 6 Squadron as 'EB'. Upgrade to GR.3A took place in 08/01 and, in the post-disbandment re-shuffle, it was allocated to 6 Squadron as 'ET'. Flown to RAF Shawbury for store 12/04/06.
XZ392	S157 F/F 13/07/77 (D. Eagles) and D/D to RAF Bruggen 17/08/77 for 31 Squadron as 'DQ'. Re-coded 'DE' by 06/79 and transferred to 20 Squadron as 'CC' by 11/83, before being handed on to 54 Squadron as 'GR' by 10/84. Upgraded to GR.1A at the JMU in 06/87 and returned to 54 Squadron as 'GQ'. Flown to RAF Shawbury for storage by 10/90, it remained in a semi-operational state until dispatch to St Athan by road on 01/12/00 for overhaul and upgrade to GR.3A. Assigned to 16 (Reserve) Squadron as 'PF' on 26/03/02, it received special marks the following year. In the post-disbandment re-shuffle it was allocated to 6 Squadron as 'EM'.
XZ393	S158 F/F 12/08/77 (E. Bucklow) and D/D to RAF Bruggen 01/09/77 for 20 Squadron as 'CP'. Transferred to 17 Squadron as 'BJ' by 06/80 and then, following attention at the JMU, to 226 OCU as '03'. Upgraded in 02/84 to GR.1A and re-assigned to 54 Squadron as 'GK', it was then lost in a crash off Cromer on 12/07/84.
XZ394	S159 F/F 02/09/77 (A. Love) and D/D to RAF Bruggen 26/09/77 for 20 Squadron as 'CQ' before being passed on to 17 Squadron as 'BJ'. Flown to RAF Shawbury for short-term storage on 20/03/85, it was shipped to the JMU in early 1987 for upgrade to GR.1A and re-issued to 6 Squadron as 'ES'. Transferred to 54 Squadron as 'GN' by 03/90, it was noted sporting the ARTF grey colour scheme in 06/93 and 09/94 for UN peacekeeping operations. Received the new permanent grey colour scheme in 07/96 and upgraded to GR.3 in 10/98 and finally to GR.3A in 11/01. In the post-disbandment re-shuffle, it was allocated to 41 Squadron as 'FG', but flown to St Athan 15/03/06.

Jaguar GR.3A XZ391 'ET' of No.6 Squadron shot over the North Sea in June 2005.

XZ395	S160 F/F 08/09/77 (E. Bucklow) and passed into store at Warton. Finally D/D to RAF Coltishall 30/01/79 for 54 Squadron, eventually taking up the code 'GN'. Transferred to 6 Squadron as 'EJ' in 05/84. Following upgrade to GR.1A at the JMU in 08/84 it had returned to 54 Squadron as 'GJ', only to be lost in a crash 30 miles north of Coltishall on 22/08/84, from which the pilot ejected successfully.
XZ396	S161 F/F 19/12/77 (E. Bucklow) and passed into storage at Warton, where it was to remain for over a year before D/D to RAF Coltishall on 23/02/79. Assigned to 6 Squadron as 'EM' but was transferred to 226 OCU as '08' by 05/84. Following upgrade to GR.1A at the JMU it was re-issued to 6 Squadron as 'EM' on 18/02/85, and was to receive the desert pink ARTF scheme for Operation Granby in 08/90, although did not participate in hostilities. It did however undertake UN peacekeeping operations, and received the ARTF grey scheme in 06/93. Given the 'stage three' modifications, it remained with 6 Squadron and received a black tail as part of the Jaguar's '25th Anniversary' marks, although this had been removed by 06/99. Taken by road to St Athan on 21/02/02 for upgrade to GR.3A, it was returned to the squadron and, in the post-disbandment re-shuffle, it was allocated the code 'EQ'. Flown to St Athan and allocated to DCAE Cosford by 03/06.
XZ397	S162 F/F 27/10/77 (P. Ginger) in primer but wearing RAF serial. Undertook four production flights and placed in store at Warton without being delivered to RAF. Identified for loan to India, it was brought up to Jaguar International standard as G-27-322 with F/F 16/11/79. Delivered to India as JI 006 on 11/12/79. Crashed while in India on 14/06/81, following a bird strike.
XZ398	S163 F/F 16/11/77 (E. Bucklow) in primer but wearing RAF serial and placed in store at Warton, never being delivered to RAF. Identified for loan to India, it was brought up to Jaguar International standard as G-27-323 and was delivered to India as JI 007 on 14/08/80. Returned to UK on 14/04/84 and was placed in short-term store again at Warton. Moved to JMU, upgraded to GR.1A, and delivered to 6 Squadron as 'EF' on 07/02/85. Transferred to 41 Squadron as 'D' in 08/87 and then to 54 Squadron as 'GA' in 06/89. Following overhaul at the JMU in early 1991, it was returned to 41 Squadron as 'A', receiving the '75th Anniversary' marking of red fin and spine and enlarged unit insignia. This was replaced by the ARTF grey scheme for overseas operations in 06/93 and then the new permanent grey scheme, which was applied at St Athan in 02/96. The jet adopted the two letter code of 'FA'. Upgraded to GR.1A, and later to GR.3 in 12/99 and then GR.3A in 04/04, it has remained with the squadron ever since.
XZ399	S164 F/F 23/11/77 (E. Bucklow) and then placed in store at Warton. Eventually D/D to RAF Coltishall 17/05/79 for use by 6 Squadron. During this period, it operated in 10/80 with a white rectangle on the fin and upper wing surfaces and the code 'EN'. Transferred to 14 Squadron as 'AG' on 10/01/83 but was back with 6 Squadron as 'EL' on 09/02/84 following attention at the JMU. Transferred to 226 OCU as code '09' by 05/84 then, following upgrade to GR.1A at the JMU in 10/85, it returned to 6 Squadron as 'EN'. Dispatched back to 226 OCU as '03' on 12/10/87, it subsequently returned to 6 Squadron as 'EJ' by 06/93, and became the Jaguar 97 trials aircraft in 02/99, and later a GR.3A when under overhaul at St Athan in 11/00. The jet remains in service with 6 Squadron as code 'EJ'.
XZ400	S165 F/F 16/02/78 (E. Bucklow) and placed in store at Warton until undertaking a re-flight on production clearance on 12/03/79 for development flying. D/D to RAF Coltishall on 29/06/79 for use by 54 Squadron. Assigned code 'GP' but spent a short period in store at RAF Abingdon. Later became the second aircraft to receive the avionics upgrade. Returned to 54 Squadron as a GR.1A on 09/12/83, and then was damaged in a landing accident at RAF Honington on 07/02/84, with the nose wheel partly retracted. Retained by 54 Squadron it had been re-coded 'GH' by 04/86 and was then transferred to 6 Squadron where it became 'EG'. Flown to RAF Shawbury for storage in 06/92, it remained here until overhaul beckoned at St Athan in 03/97. It emerged in the new grey colour scheme, and returned to 54 Squadron as 'GR'. Upgraded to GR.3 at St Athan in 05/00, it was then dispatched to Warton to participate in the RR/Adour 106 engine upgrade trials. It returned to RAF Coltishall on 24/01/02 as the first production aircraft with the upgraded engine. Transferred to 41 Squadron as 'FQ' in the post-disbandment re-shuffle. It was flown to St Athan on 06/07/05 where it has been wfu.
ZB615	B38 F/F 23/09/82 (Aitken/Hurst) as a T.2A and delivered to 5 MU RAF Kemble on 16/11/82 for repainting in the RAE red/white/blue corporate colour scheme. Assigned initially to the RAE at Farnborough, and then the DTEO-FJTS and ETPS. It was retired from use in 11/05.

CHAPTER 5
EXPORT JAGUARS

ROYAL AIR FORCE OF OMAN
(formerly The Sultan of Oman Air Force)

Oman was one of two anonymous export customers announced on 28 August 1974. The order was to comprise twelve Jaguar Internationals, together with a pair of two-seat trainers. Deliveries commenced in March 1977 to equip a single squadron, No.8, at Masirah, identifiable by their red badge. Deliveries were undertaken by company pilots via Toulouse and Akrotiri.

A follow-on order was received for a further batch of aircraft in mid-1982, by which time two aircraft, one single-seat and one dual, had been lost in accidents. As an attrition replacement for the twin-seater, XX138, which was on loan to India, was sold, at the completion of its lease, directly to Oman. The aircraft was later flown to the UK for overhaul by the JMU at Abingdon between September and December 1983.

The second batch of aircraft to equip 20 Squadron (blue badge), at the same base began being delivered in May 1983, with deliveries being completed by November. The two twin-seaters ordered, 213 and 214, were unique in having the same ARI 18223 RWR as the single-seat versions and in being the only Warton-built aircraft to have French-type fixed in-flight refuelling probes.

Attrition of a further five aircraft over the next decade saw a further two ex-RAF examples purchased, although both of these were brought up to Jaguar 96 configuration. The remaining RAFO fleet has since returned to Warton for overhaul and upgrade to a similar standard in a £40 million deal. This was followed in September 1997 by a further upgrade for a similar figure, to be undertaken in Oman.

Jaguars of the Royal Air Force of Oman:

200	T.2, ex-XX138, JI 001.
201	OB G–27–278, F/F 04/11/76 (E. Bucklow/V. Malings), D/D 07/03/77. W/O 01/03/81, 22 miles north of Thumrait.
202	OS G–27–280, F/F 27/01/77 (J. Lee), D/D 07/03/77, G–BEET.
203	OB G–27–279, F/F 06/04/77 (A. Love//J. Evans) D/D 27/06/77, G–BETB.
204	OS G–27–281, F/F 18/05/77 (E. Bucklow), D/D 27/06/77.
205	OS G–27–282, F/F 18/08/77 (A. Love), D/D 26/09/77. W/O 27/10/91, 5 miles south of Masirah.
206	OS G–27–283, F/F 19/08/77 (T. Ferguson), D/D 26/09/77.
207	OS G–27–284, F/F 07/10/77 (E. Bucklow), D/D 07/11/77. W/O 17/12/91, west of Jebel range.

Seven 'RAFO' Jaguar Internationals await delivery at Warton.

A four ship of 'RAFO' Jaguar Internationals in close formation over the Omani desert.

FUERZA AEREA ECUATORIANA

Ecuador was the second undisclosed recipient of the two orders for Jaguar announced on 28 August 1974. The order was to comprise two twin-seaters and ten singles, arising out of a visit and examination of the aircraft by the Commander-in-Chief of the FAE in September 1972.

These were all delivered by BAC/BAE SYSTEMS crews during 1977 to equip Escuadron de Combate 2111 as a component of Grupo 211, flying out of Ala de Combate 21 at Base Aerea Militar Taura, near Guaysquil.

FAE302 Jaguar International of the Fuerza Aerea Ecuatoriana.

208	OS G-27-285, F/F 14/10/77 (E. Bucklow), D/D 07/11/77. W/O 31/12/85.
209	OS G-27-286, F/F 16/12/77 (E. Bucklow), D/D 06/02/78.
210	OS G-27-287, F/F 12/01/78 (P. Ginger), D/D 06/02/78.
211	OS G-27-288, F/F 08/03/78 (E.Bucklow), D/D 08/05/78.
212	OS G-27-289, F/F 31/03/78 (E. Bucklow), D/D 08/05/78. W/O 26/02/79 after bomb exploded.
213	OB G-27-375, F/F 05/11/82 (S. Aitken/K. Hartley), D/D 23/05/83.
214	OB G-27-376, F/F 26/11/82 (P. Orme/L. Hurst), D/D 25/07/83.
215	OS G-27-377, F/F 15/09/82 (E. Bucklow), D/D 23/05/83.
216	OS G-27-378, F/F 02/11/82 (S. Aitken), D/D 23/05/83. W/O 29/01/91, 40 miles north-east of Thumrait.
217	OS G-27-379, F/F 07/01/83 (S. Aitken), D/D 25/07/83.
218	OS G-27-380, F/F 12/05/83 (C. Yeo), D/D 25/07/83. W/O 21/06/84.
219	OS G-27-381, F/F 26/04/83 (E. Bucklow), D/D 19/09/83.
220	OS G-27-382, F/F 18/05/83 (C. Yeo), D/D 19/09/83.
221	OS G-27-383, F/F 01/06/83 (P. Orme), D/D 19/09/83.
222	OS G-27-384, F/F 15/06/83 (P. Gordon-Johnson), D/D 24/11/83.
223	OS G-27-385, F/F 07/07/83 (E. Bucklow), D/D 24/11/83.
224	OS G-27-386, F/F 15/07/83 (E. Bucklow), D/D 24/11/83.
225	GR.1, ex-XX740, JI 017, D/D 04/11/86.
226	GR.1, ex-XX719, D/D 10/08/98.

Below Aircraft identification can be confusing. FAE283 seen here on a test flight from Warton displaying the code EB1 (first twin-seat for Ecuador), PS168 (the 168th Jaguar produced) and G-27-266 (its UK 'B' registration for flight testing).

Attrition has accounted for four of the aircraft and BAE SYSTEMS had at one point been on the brink of supplying replacements; a number of aircraft were transported from store at RAF Shawbury to Warton, including XX121 and XX722. However, by July 1993 these had returned to store, presumably following the failure of the company to secure an order.

In 2000, Esc 2111 was still operating six aircraft, with two others, 339 and 348, in long-term store.

283	EB G–27–266, F/F 19/08/76 (T. Ferguson/J. Evans), D/D 04/01/77.
289	ES G–27–268, F/F 28/09/76 (P. Millett), D/D 04/01/77. W/O 29/03/90 or 13/06/90, 34 km from Guaysquil.
302	ES G–27–269, F/F 14/12/76 (E. Bucklow), D/D 31/05/77.
305	EB G–27–267, F/F 07/01/77 (E. Bucklow/R. Taylor), D/D 31/05/77.
309	ES G–27–270, F/F 08/02/77 (P. Ginger), D/D 18/04/77.
318	ES G–27–271, F/F 25/02/77 (R. Stock), D/D 18/04/77. W/O 16/08/88.
327	ES G–27–272, F/F 01/04/77 (E. Bucklow), D/D 16/08/77.
329	ES G–27–273, F/F 26/04/77 (E. Bucklow), D/D 16/08/77.
339	ES G–27–274, F/F 05/07/77 (R. Stock), D/D 05/09/77.
340	ES G–27–275, F/F 04/08/77 (E. Bucklow), D/D 05/09/77. W/O 22/10/89.
348	ES G–27–276, F/F 19/09/77 (E. Bucklow), D/D 24/10/77.
349	ES G–27–277, F/F 27/09/77 (E. Bucklow), D/D 24/10/77. W/O 16/09/81 when struck mountain.

NIGERIAN AIR FORCE

Nigeria became the fourth and last export customer for the Jaguar. The country agreed in early 1983 to go ahead with the purchase of eighteen examples, with an option of a further eighteen. In July 1983, the Government ratified the first batch, and the handover of four single-seat and four twin-seat aircraft occurred at Warton on 11 May 1984.

Initial pilot training had been undertaken by the RAF through 226 OCU at RAF Lossiemouth with follow-on training being managed by BAE SYSTEMS at Warton. All the aircraft to Nigeria were delivered between September 1984 and June 1985 and used to equip a single squadron at Makurdi. Losses appear to include one twin-seater and three single-seaters, one of which was severely damaged in a ground accident when it jumped chocks.

Nigerian Air Force Jaguar International NAF705 seen during a test flight from Warton.

Farnborough 1984 and Nigerian Air Force Jaguar International NAF710/G-27-397.

In 1991, barely six years after delivery, the Jaguars were taken out of service due to the economical situation affecting Nigeria. The surviving fourteen aircraft (ten SN and four BN) have remained in store ever since.

700	NB G-27-387, F/F 13/10/83 (E. Bucklow/A. Aitken), D/D 18/09/84.
701	NB G-27-388, F/F 02/11/83 (A. Aitken/Blagborough), D/D 25/09/84.
702	NB G-27-389, F/F 22/11/83 (A. Aitken/Dix), D/D 30/10/84. W/O 26/04/85.
703	NB G-27-390, F/F 01/03/84 (A. Aitken/Holder), D/D 20/08/84.
704	NB G-27-391, F/F 18/04/84 (E. Bucklow/Hurst), D/D 11/12/84.
705	NS G-27-392, F/F 21/12/83 (A. Aitken), D/D 20/08/84.
706	NS G-27-393, F/F 10/01/84 (E. Bucklow), D/D 28/08/84.
707	NS G-27-394, F/F 03/02/84 (A. Aitken), D/D 28/08/84.
708	NS G-27-395, F/F 28/03/84 (C. Yeo), D/D 18/09/84.
709	NS G-27-396, F/F 11/05/84 (A. Aitken), D/D 25/09/84.
710	NS G-27-397, F/F 18/06/84 (C. Yeo), D/D 30/10/84.
711	NS G-27-398, F/F 18/07/84 (C. Yeo), D/D 11/12/84.
712	NS G-27-399, F/F 07/09/84 (A. Aitken), D/D 10/04/85.
713	NS G-27-400, F/F 01/11/84 (P. Orme), D/D 10/04/85.
714	NS G-27-401, F/F 14/12/84 (C. Yeo), D/D 04/06/85. W/O 14/07/85 or 25/07/85.
715	NS G-27-402, F/F 12/02/85 (E. Bucklow), D/D 04/06/85.
716	NS G-27-403, F/F 11/03/85 (E. Bucklow), D/D 25/06/85.
717	NS G-27-404, F/F 01/05/85 (C. Yeo), D/D 25/06/85.

Jaguar T.2 XX143 in guise of JI 002 at RAF Abingdon shortly after its return from loan to the Indian Air Force. The aircraft was later lost in a crash on 18 September 1986.

INDIAN AIR FORCE/BHARATIYA VAYU SENA

India became the third export customer for the Jaguar and is likely to be both the last and possibly the biggest user.

As with most negotiations that take place in India, the sale was a protracted state of affairs and nearly stalled more than once. Beginning with first expressions of interest as early as 1966 and Wing Commander Prithi Singh having soloed in XW560 in June 1972, the deal was not finally settled until twelve years later. In early 1975 an order for fifty aircraft was vetoed because India was requesting an unusually low rate. At the same time an approach by Libya for thirty-nine aircraft was also vetoed while interest from Turkey for twenty-four and Saudi Arabia for eighty to 100 came to nothing. The following year, Pakistan's interest in an initial order of six aircraft foundered on funding difficulties.

Finally, in September 1978 India selected Jaguar to meet its deep strike capability, with a requirement of 200 aircraft. These were to be ordered in batches of twenty, with the initial forty to be built at Warton, and the remainder under licence.

Given the leisurely pace of this decision, the urgency to get the aircraft into squadron service was almost indecent. This resulted in the loan of eighteen RAF aircraft to equip No.14 Squadron at Ambala. These loan aircraft consisted of sixteen Jaguar GR.1 (interim) and two Jaguar T.2 (interim) aircraft.

The forty Warton-produced aircraft were of a similar standard to the current RAF jets, with Adour Mk 804E engines and NAVWASS avionics. The first delivery took place on 21 February 1981, with completion of the order in November 1982. These replaced the former RAF aircraft on loan to 14 Squadron, but only after its co-located No.5 Squadron had been equipped.

The first 'batch three' aircraft, JS136, built from Anglo-French kits by HAL at Bangalore, undertook its first flight on 31 March 1982 and, although the air force was to equip a further three squadrons, including No.6 at Poona (fitted with the nose-mounted Agave radar for anti-shipping duties) and 16 and 27 Squadrons at Gorakhpur, the story, with its political meanderings, is perhaps for volume two.

JI 001	Ex-XX138, G-27-320, D/D 23/07/79. Sold to SOAF 1982.
JI 002	Ex-XX143, G-27-321, D/D 14/10/79. Returned to UK 09/09/82.
JI 003	Ex-XX720, G-27-319, D/D 23/07/79. Returned to UK 24/02/84.
JI 004	Ex-XX117, G-27-317, D/D 14/10/79. Returned to UK 24/02/84.

JI 005	Ex-XX115, G-27-315, D/D 11/12/79. Returned to UK 23/07/82.
JI 006	Ex-XZ397, G-27-322, D/D 11/12/79. W/O 16/04/81.
JI 007	Ex-XZ398, G-27-323, D/D 14/08/80. Returned to UK 19/04/84.
JI 008	Ex-XX116, G-27-316, D/D 11/12/79. Returned to UK 19/04/84.
JI 009	Ex-XX728, G-27-324, D/D 29/04/80. Returned to UK 23/07/82.
JI 010	Ex-XX725, G-27-325, D/D 13/02/80. Returned to UK 19/04/84.
JI 011	Ex-XX111, G-27-314, D/D 13/02/80. W/O 10/04/82.
JI 012	Ex-XX729, G-27-326, D/D 29/04/80. Returned to UK 25/05/82.
JI 013	Ex-XX736, G-27-327, D/D 13/02/80. Returned to UK 24/02/84.
JI 014	Ex-XX734, G-27-328, D/D 14/08/80. Returned to UK 11/02/82.
JI 015	Ex-XX737, G-27-330, D/D 14/08/80. Returned to UK 25/05/82.
JI 016	Ex-XX738, G-27-329, D/D 13/02/80. Returned to UK 19/04/84.
JI 017	Ex-XX740, G-27-331, D/D 14/08/80. Returned to UK 19/04/84.
JI 018	Ex-XX118, G-27-318, D/D 11/12/79. Returned to UK 25/05/82.
JT 051	G-27-368 F/F 01/09/80 (E. Bucklow/G. McAuley), D/D 21/02/81.
JT 052	G-27-369 F/F 08/10/80 (C. Yeo/P. Kelly), D/D 21/02/81.
JT 053	G-27-370 F/F 04/12/81 (J.J. Lee/D. Thomas), D/D 21/02/81.
JT 054	G-27-371 F/F 05/08/81 (S. Aitken), D/D 16/09/81.
JT 055	G-27-372 F/F 18/11/81 (K. Hartley/J. Stuttard), D/D 30/01/82.
JS 101	G-27-333 F/F 17/02/81 (P. Gordon-Johnson), D/D 01/07/81.
JS 102	G-27-334 F/F 22/04/81 (P. Orme), D/D 01/07/81.
JS 103	G-27-335 F/F 01/06/81 (P. Orme), D/D 16/09/81
JS 104	G-27-336 F/F 02/07/81 (S. Aitken), D/D 16/09/81. W/O 1/06/84.
JS 105	G-27-337 F/F 28/08/81 (S. Aitken), D/D 20/09/81.
JS 106	G-27-338 F/F 18/09/81 (S. Aitken), D/D 20/09/81.
JS 107	G-27-339 F/F 06/10/81 (S. Aitken), D/D 17/12/81.
JS 108	G-27-340 F/F 22/10/81 (P. Orme), D/D 17/12/81.
JS 109	G-27-341 F/F 28/10/81 (S. Aitken), D/D 17/12/81.
JS 110	G-27-342 F/F 09/11/81 (S. Aitken), D/D 17/12/81.
JS 111	G-27-343 F/F 02/12/81 (S. Aitken), D/D 30/01/82. W/O 22/02/85.
JS 112	G-27-344 F/F 05/12/81 (S. Aitken), D/D 30/01/82.
JS 113	G-27-345 F/F 17/12/81 (E. Bucklow), D/D 30/01/82.
JS 114	G-27-346 F/F 13/01/82 (S. Aitken), D/D 18/03/82. W/O 12/04/84.
JS 115	G-27-347 F/F 20/01/81 (P. Orme), D/D 18/03/82.
JS 116	G-27-348 F/F 27/01/82 (S. Aitken), D/D 18/03/82.
JS 117	G-27-349 F/F 08/02/82 (S. Aitken), D/D 18/03/82.
JS 118	G-27-350 F/F 16/02/82 (E. Bucklow), D/D 22/04/82.
JS 119	G-27-351 F/F 22/02/82 (P. Orme), D/D 22/04/82.
JS 120	G-27-352 F/F 02/03/82 (J.J. Lee), D/D 22/04/82.
JS 121	G-27-353 F/F 16/03/82 (P. Orme), D/D 22/04/82.
JS 122	G-27-354 F/F 20/03/82 (S. Aitken), D/D 14/06/82. W/O 07/08/84.
JS 123	G-27-355 F/F 05/04/82 (S. Aitken), D/D 14/06/82.
JS 124	G-27-356 F/F 27/03/82 (S. Aitken), D/D 14/06/82.
JS 125	G-27-357 F/F 14/04/82 (S. Aitken), D/D 14/06/82. W/O 19/10/80.

Indian Air Force JI 004, a la XX117.

A line-up of eleven Indian Air Force Jaguar Internationals prior to delivery at Warton.

JS 126	G-27-358 F/F 21/04/82 (P. Gordon-Johnson), D/D 09/08/82.
JS 127	G-27-359 F/F 05/05/82 (P. Orme), D/D 09/08/82.
JS 128	G-27-360 F/F 07/05/82 (S. Aitken), D/D 09/08/82.
JS 129	G-27-361 F/F 20/05/82 (S. Aitken), D/D 09/08/82.
JS 130	G-27-362 F/F 24/05/82 (P. Orme), D/D 24/09/82.
JS 131	G-27-363 F/F 10/06/82 (P. Orme), D/D 24/09/82.
JS 132	G-27-364 F/F 16/06/82 (P. Orme), D/D 24/09/82.
JS 133	G-27-365 F/F 29/06/82 (S. Aitken), D/D 06/11/82.
JS 134	G-27-366 F/F 09/07/82 (P. Orme), D/D 24/09/82.
JS 135	G-27-367 F/F 28/07/82 (E. Bucklow), D/D 06/11/82.

CHAPTER 6

A TEST PILOT'S LIFE IS NOT ALWAYS A DULL ONE

An interview with Eric Bucklow on the delivery of two Jaguar Internationals to Ecuador

The RAF, most of the Omanis and ultimately the Indian Jaguars were all delivered predominantly by their own crews. The Ecuadorian aircraft were, however, delivered by our own production test pilots as part of the contract. I delivered one, FAE 329, with J. Cockburn in the second aircraft, FAE 327. It was an interesting delivery. Because of the relatively short range of the aircraft, we had to go to some strange places in west Africa to get round to the jumping off point for Ascension Island. All together, there were ten legs between Warton and Taura.

Liberia was one of the more unusual staging posts, and I think at one place we broke into the circuit as the locals were about to have

FAE Jaguar Internationals 327 and 329 lift off from Warton's runway on 16 August 1977 at the start of the long flight to Taura.

an insurrection and I think they thought that these arrivals, these military aircraft, with a whiz and a roar into the circuit, signalled the start of the insurrection. I do not think the insurrection went too well after that, probably because of the timing! Apparently we nearly got shot at again as we departed because of these people being a bit trigger-happy.

We eventually got out to Ascension – Ascension is actually owned by Great Britain but there is a big US air force base, a staging post; it is also the down range point for the missile launches from Cape Canaveral and I think they were looking at things like 'Mervs' at that stage. When we got out of the aeroplanes, the ground crew said: 'you are invited to a party. The Station Commander would like you to come.' We thought that was very nice of him, so we turned up at this party and were greeted with a couple of Tequilas with salt round the edge. When I asked for an orange juice, I was looked at rather strangely. At about 11 o'clock we decided to go to bed, as we had to be up early the next day, me and the chap flying the other one. We went to find the Station Commander who was sitting on the ground drinking with his friends. I bent down and said 'thank you very much for the party, Sir' and he rose to say goodbye and it was rather like one of those V2 rocket sequences which goes wrong where he rises to a full height and then crashes to the ground. He was obviously extremely the worse for wear but we then found out that he had a party every night, so there was nothing special about inviting us to this one.

We then went to the Met Office and it was quite critical for the Ascension to Recife leg; I think it was about 1,220 miles. The safe range of the Jaguar was not that much more. We couldn't tolerate a headwind to be safe and therefore we were quite interested in the Met and were very impressed when we received this great read-out which came from the Cape which detailed winds and temperatures not every 5,000ft as the British Met Office would do, but every 1,000ft. I thought – gosh this is super stuff, but unfortunately it was just as wrong as the 5,000 stuff often is.

We were OK but the first pair of aircraft that went out there got a similar forecast, which was wrong, and they finished up quite short of fuel.

We got out eventually to Ecuador and we arrived at Taura Air Force Base down in the south, which is quite close to Guayquil. However, because there were no customs facilities at Taura, we had to go to Guayquil to get out passports stamped as having entered the country as, if we came to depart the country and we hadn't been stamped in, there was no way we would have got out. We were met by our BAE representative, a chap called Paul, who took us to the airport and, when we got there, being an aircraft spotter, I asked whether it would be OK if I walk along and take all the numbers of the many aircraft there. He said: 'yes, fine, keep your red flying suit on'. We used to have red flying suits then, with gold bars, like an airline captain, to help get us through customs. He said, if anybody asks what you are doing, just say 'Piloto Hagua' and they will think you are a God. Unfortunately the three dogs I encountered at one of the little agricultural aircraft yards did not know I was a God. I managed to ward off two of them with a telescope, but the third one got round behind me and bit my ankle.

I went back to Paul and told him I had been bitten by an Ecuadorean dog. He said: 'Oh dear we had better go and find the Ecuadorean Air Force doctor.' They had a transport guy on the base who said we would have to keep an eye on this dog for ten days and, if it got rabies in that time, then I would also. At that time they were not keen on doing the injection which was a fairly nasty affair into the stomach. We got the Ecuadorean Air Force doctor who was quite willing, so we took him to the place. He thought it might be difficult to establish which dog it was but then the fast approach of a dust cloud solved that problem and, at some danger of being bitten himself, he undertook to check every day to see how it was getting on.

As we drove out of this particular place we crossed over one of their open sewers with rats climbing up the side, so I thought the dog was bound to have rabies.

I went off aircraft spotting in America and forgot about this. Meanwhile, my mate who had flown the other aircraft out went straight home. When he got home, he went round to my wife and said if she heard that I had been bitten by an Ecuadorean dog, don't worry. Well she hadn't, so she did. I then eventually got home and the dog had been looked at for ten days and she did not

Jaguar GR.1 XX113, lost near Malvern on 17 July 1981 on a test flight from RAF Abingdon following overhaul. Fl. Lt Kenuyn ejected safely.

Eric Bucklow's log book detailing the legs of the delivery of FAE327 and 329.

have rabies, which was very surprising. My friends in Flight Ops reckoned that, as I was fairly thin at that time, the dog thought I was a big red juicy bone.

Jaguar T.2 XX136 seen leaving Warton on a development flight with a centre-line external fuel tank and a mixed bomb load. The jet was lost on its 236th flight near Wimborne St Giles with the crew of Wing Commander Austin and Fl. Lt Cruikshanks ejecting safely.

CHAPTER 7
JAGUAR ATTRITION

Accident Date	Aircraft serial/code	Unit	Details
26/03/70	E01	CEAM	Crashed on single-engined approach to Istres following a fire in the No.2 engine. Total time: 130 hours.
14/02/72	A03	CEAM	Written-off following heavy landing at Tarnos, France.
11/08/72	XW560	A&AEE	Written off in a ground fire at Boscombe Down.
22/11/74	XX136	A&AEE	Crashed at Wimborne St Giles.
25/03/75	E26	SEPECAT	Crashed on a pre-delivery test flight, 16 miles north-east of Reims, France.
30/04/75	XX831 'W'	226 OCU	Crashed at RAF Lossiemouth.
02/07/85	E34	Esc	Crashed.
06/02/76	XX137 'A'	226 OCU	Crashed into the Moray Firth after running out of fuel following a leak in the low pressure system.
02/07/76	XX822 'AA'	14 Sqn	Crashed 15 miles west of Alhorn, West Germany.
15/09/76	XX735	6 Sqn	Crashed near to Eggebek, West Germany, during Exercise Teamwork 76.
17/09/76	XX120	54 Sqn	Crashed into the sea off Samsoe Island, Denmark, during Exercise Teamwork 76.
14/12/76	XZ102 'H'	II (AC) Sqn	Crashed 10km north-east of Laarbruch.
14/01/77	A71 '11-MB'	11 Esc	Crashed near to Villers-sous-Preny, France.
14/02/77	A18	7 Esc	Crashed near Troyes, France.
25/02/77	XZ120	II (AC) Sqn	Crashed into North Sea, Nordholm, Denmark.
14/06/77	XX978 'DM'	31 Sqn	Crashed near Verden, West Germany.
29/07/77	XX148 'M'	226 OCU	Crashed at Whittingham, UK.
21/03/78	XX971 'DE'	31 Sqn	Crashed on take-off from CFB Lahr, West Germany.
27/04/78	XX149 'N'	226 OCU	Crashed into a mountain near Banff, Scotland, en-route from Coltishall to Lossiemouth.
03/05/78		11 Esc	Shot down by Polisario guerillas in Mauritania.
31/05/78	A52	11 Esc	Crashed in Chad.
06/06/78	XX761 '11'	226 OCU	Written-off in a ground fire at RAF Lossiemouth.
21/07/78	E14	7 Esc	Crashed.
25/07/78	XX823 'BG'	17 Sqn	Flew into a hill during armament practice camp while on detachment to Decimomannu, Sardinia.
08/08/78	A109	11 Esc	Crashed near Ati, Chad, while on a reconnaissance flight.
23/08/78	A111	11 Esc	Crashed following a mid-air collision with another Jaguar 400km from Ndjamena, Chad.
14/10/78	A106	11 Esc	Crashed at Ndjamena, Chad.
01/11/78	XX759 '19'	226 OCU	Crashed near Selkirk, killing the Ecuadorean pilot.
26/02/79	212	8 Sqn	Crashed near Thumrait, Oman, during a firepower demonstration, after a bomb exploded beneath the wing.
26/03/79	XX147 'BY'	17 Sqn	Crashed near to Sudlohn, Borken, West Germany, following a bird strike.
20/06/79	A62 '3-XI'	3 Esc	Crashed near Nancy, France.
22/06/79	XX142 'G'	226 OCU	Crashed in the Moray Firth, 10 miles north of Lossiemouth.
12/07/79	A45 '7-IB'	7 Esc	Crashed at Norvenich, West Germany.
17/07/79		Esc	Crashed at Siegenburg, West Germany.
18/07/79	XX960 'AK'	14 Sqn	Crashed near Iserlohn, West Germany.
23/11/79	XX762 '28'	226 OCU	Crashed 2,000ft up Beinn a'Chleibh mountain, near Dalmally, Argyllshire.
10/12/79	XX749 '21'	226 OCU	Crashed near Lumsden, Aberdeenshire, following a mid-air collision with XX755.
10/12/79	XX755 '08'	226 OCU	Crashed near Lumsden, Aberdeenshire, following a mid-air collision with XX749.
28/05/80	XX964 'BL'	17 Sqn	Crashed at Bruggen following a mid-air collision with XX961 during the landing break.
28/05/80	XX961 'BJ'	17 Sqn	Crashed at Bruggen following a mid-air collision with XX964 during the landing break.
17/07/80	XX817 'BB'	17 Sqn	Crashed into woods, 7 miles from Bruggen.
05/02/81	A68 '3-XG'	3 Esc	Crashed at Nancy-Ochey, France.
12/02/81	XX827 'BM'	17 Sqn	Crashed on Nellis Range during a 'Red Flag' exercise. 31 Sqn pilot.

The Germany-based squadrons seemed to fare quite badly in the attrition stakes. Another loss on 28 May 1980 occurred when XX961 and XX964 collided in the overhead at RAF Bruggen. The latter is seen here at the same location a year earlier on 21 June 1979.

Above Another RAF Germany loss was Jaguar GR.1 XX973 'DG' of No.31 Squadron. This jet crashed on 14 April 1981 some four miles south-west of Gutersloh.

Below XX957 'CG' of No.20 Squadron crashed on 21 October 1981 after being struck by lightning when on finals to RAF Bruggen. Fl. Lt Prestcott ejected safely. It is seen here at the same location on 21 June 1979.

01/03/81	201	8 Sqn	Crashed 22 miles north of Thumrait.
18/03/81	A63	11 Esc	Crashed 14km north of Toul, France.
14/04/81	XX973 'DG'	31 Sqn	Crashed 4 miles north-west of Gutersloh, West Germany.
16/04/81	JI 006	IAF	Crashed following a bird strike.
01/06/81	XX828 'P'	226 OCU	Crashed 5 miles north of Forfar, near Kurriemuir.
13/06/81	A51	Esc	Crashed.
17/07/81	XX113 '09'	226 OCU	Crashed near to Malvern.
24/07/81	XX916	ETPS	Crashed into Bristol Channel, 12 miles off Hartland Point.
06/08/81	XX972 'DF'	31 Sqn	Crashed at Barnard Castle, Co. Durham.
16/09/81	349	Esc 2111	Crashed in Ecuador after striking a mountain top.
21/10/81	XX957 'CG'	20 Sqn	Crashed on approach to Bruggen after a lightning strike.
18/11/81	XX758 '18'	226 OCU	Crashed 14 miles west of Dingwall.
10/03/82	A114	Esc	Crashed.
02/04/82	XX122 'GA'	54 Sqn	Crashed into the wash off Heacham, Norfolk.
10/04/82	JI 011	IAF	Crashed.
26/04/82	A30	Esc	Crashed.
25/05/82	XX963 'AL'	14 Sqn	Crashed near Wesel, West Germany, after the accidental firing of a Sidewinder missile by a Phantom FGR.2 of 92 Sqn.
11/06/82	XX820 'BD'	17 Sqn	Crashed on final approach to Bruggen.
25/06/82	A134	Esc	Crashed.
01/07/82	A42	11 Esc	Crashed after leaving the runway at Bordeaux.
07/07/82	A77	7 Esc	Crashed on take-off from St Dizier.
13/09/82	XX760 'AA'	14 Sqn	Crashed 2 miles north of Braegrudie, near Rogart, Sutherland.
14/09/82	A155	Esc	Crashed.
29/09/82	XX768 'BA'	17 Sqn	Crashed at Heinsberg-Randerath, north-east of Geilenkirchen, West Germany.
07/03/83	XZ376 'BE'	17 Sqn	Crashed on the Tain range, Scotland.
05/04/83	A105 '11–EV'	11 Esc	Crashed near Bapaume.
19/04/83	XX742 'EF'	6 Sqn	Crashed into the North Sea, 40 miles off Bacton, Norfolk.
16/06/83	XZ105 '25'	2 (AC) Sqn	Crashed after colliding with XZ110 in Labrador while operating from CFB Goose Bay.
16/06/83	XZ110 '30'	2 (AC) Sqn	Crashed after colliding with XZ105 in Labrador while operating from CFB Goose Bay.
22/06/83	XX721 'GE'	54 Sqn	Crashed near Hahn, West Germany.
27/07/83	A6 '3-XH'	3 Esc	Crashed on take-off from Nancy-Ochey.
16/08/83	A102 '11–YK'	11 Esc	Crashed near Saintes.
19/09/83	XX114 '02'	226 OCU	Crashed on take-off from Lossiemouth.
19/10/83	JS 125	IAF	Crashed.
10/01/84	A143	11 Esc	Crashed near Metz.
17/01/84	XX915	ETPS	Crashed on Porton Down, Wiltshire.
25/01/84	A81	11 Esc	Crashed in Chad.
07/02/84	XX750 'AL'	14 Sqn	Crashed on Nellis range, Nevada, during a 'Red Flag' exercise.

Perhaps the most infamous Jaguar loss was that of XX963 'AL' of No.14 Squadron when it was inadvertently shot down by an AIM-9 sidewinder missile fired by the crew of No.92 Squadron Phantom FGR.2 XV422 'O on 25 May 1982. The jet came down near Wesel, West Germany, with the pilot ejecting safely. It was reported at the time that he had been unaware of the missile strike and had put the cause down to a colossal engine malfunction. Well, he wasn't wrong there!

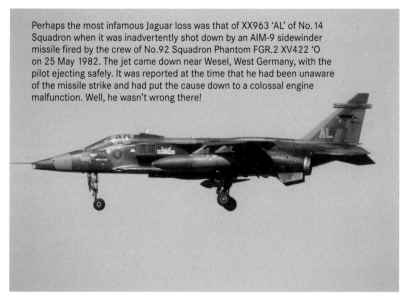

Jaguar GR.1 XX750 '22' 226 OCU seen at RAF Lossiemouth on 20 August 1975. It crashed later whilst in the service of No.14 Squadron whilst participating in a Red Flag exercise over the Nellis Range. The pilot, Fl. Lt Jackson, was unfortunately killed.

20/03/84	A69	7 Esc	Crashed in Coiron Moutains near Montelimar following a mid-air collision with a Mirage IIIE of EC.13.
30/03/84	A78 '7-HM'	7 Esc	Crashed.
11/04/84 or 12/04/84	JS 114	IAF	Crashed.
16/04/84	A125		Crashed in northern Chad.
11/05/84	A57		Crashed at Istres following fuel contamination.
01/06/84	JS 104	IAF	Crashed.
21/06/84	218	20 Sqn	Crashed.
12/07/84	XZ393 'GK'	54 Sqn	Crashed into North Sea near Cromer after colliding with TWCU Tornado GR.1 ZA408.
07/08/84	JS 122	IAF	Crashed.
22/08/84	XZ395 'GJ'	54 Sqn	Crashed into North Sea, 30 miles north of Coltishall.
05/12/84	A147 '11-EB'	11 Esc	Crashed, and pilot killed.
13/02/85	A132 '11-EA'	11 Esc	Crashed.
22/02/85 or 01/03/85	JS 110	IAF	Crashed.
01/04/85	XZ388 'AH'	14 Sqn	Crashed near Rebberlah, north-east of Celle, West Germany.
26/04/85	702	NAF	Crashed.
10/07/85	XZ365 '33'	2 (AC) Sqn	Crashed near Meschede, east of Dortmund, West Germany.
14/07/85 or 25/07/85	714	NAF	Crashed in western Nigeria, and pilot killed.

07/10/85	XX728 'EH'	6 Sqn	Crashed after colliding with XX731 in the Hartside Pass, Cumbria.
07/10/85	XX731 'ED'	6 Sqn	Crashed after colliding with XX728 in the Hartside Pass, Cumbria.
17/10/85	A136 '11-E_'	11 Esc	Crashed in the Alps, 20 miles from Grenoble.
17/10/85	A156 '11-EM'	11 Esc	Crashed in the Alps, 20 miles from Grenoble.
31/12/85	208	8 Sqn	Crashed.
03/01/86	A85 '11-MG'	11 Esc	Crashed near the dam of Le Poset, Doubs.
27/03/86	A152	Esc	Crashed on take-off at Bangui, Central Afrtican Republic.
30/06/86	A116 '11-MN'	11 Esc	Crashed at Kleine Brogel following a mid-air collision with Belgian AF F-16A FA79.
27/11/86	XX732 '03'	226 OCU	Crashed on Stocks Hill in the Craik Forest, 11 miles south-west of Hawick, killing the USAF exchange pilot.
30/01/87	A20 '7-NN'	7 Esc	Crashed near Cadenet (Vaucluse), France.
17/06/87	XZ116 'D'	41 Sqn	Crashed following a head-on collision with Tornado GR.1 ZA493 'GH', 20 Sqn, in the Borrowdale Valley, Cumbria.
24/06/87	XZ386 '05'	226 OCU	Crashed into a hillside near Aberedu, Powys, Wales.
20/08/87	E33	Esc	Crashed close to a café at Baux de Provence.
30/08/87		IAF	Crashed at Koonoor, India.
06/10/87	A60	Esc	Crashed.
02/11/87	A121	Esc	Crashed.
18/11/87	XX758 '18'	226 OCU	Crashed 14 miles west of Dingwall, Scotland.
18/04/88	A146	Esc	Crashed.

XZ116 'D' of No.41 (F) Squadron was involved in a head-on mid-air collision with No.20 Squadron Tornado GR.1 ZA493 'GH' in the Borrowdale Valley, Cumbria, on 17 June 1987. As a result of this came the introduction of flow routes in the low-level flying areas. The jet is seen at Coltishall in happier times on 11 January 1983.

07/06/88	A110 '11-EJ'	11 Esc	Crashed north-east of Orleans following a mid-air collision with another Jaguar over Puiseaux.
07/08/88	XX834 'EZ'	6 Sqn	Crashed near Wildbad-Kreuth, West Germany, after striking high-tension cables while operating from Hahn.
16/08/88	318	Esc 2111	Crashed in Ecuador.
29/03/89		NAF	Crashed and pilot killed.
13/04/89	XZ359 'M'	41 Sqn	Crashed after hitting cliffs 6 miles north-east of St Abbs Head, Berwick.
06/06/89		Aircraft System Test	Crashed at Barur (Tamil Nadu), India, and pilot killed.
22/10/89	340	Esc 2111	Crashed in Ecuador.
23/10/89	E31 '7-PE'	7 Esc	Crashed near St Eulien, north-west of St Dizier.
06/11/89	A56 '7-HD'	7 Esc	Crashed near Vitry-le-Francois.
13/06/90 or 29/03/90	289	Esc 2111	Crashed 34km from Guaysquil, Ecuador.
01/08/90		IAF	Crashed near Deoria, Utter Prudesh, following a mid-air collision with another Jaguar.
01/08/90		IAF	Crashed near Deoria, Utter Prudesh, following a mid-air collision with another Jaguar.
13/11/90	XX754		Crashed in Qatar 100 miles south of Bahrain in build-up period to the Gulf War.
12/09/90	XZ387 'GG'	54 Sqn	Crashed in the Solway Firth, 5 miles off Southerness Point, Dumfries & Galloway, Scotland.
17/01/91	A91 '11-YG'	11 Esc	Damaged beyond economical repair over Iraq.
29/01/91	216	20 Sqn	Crashed in open desert 40 miles north-east of Thumrait.
04/02/91	A10 '11-YH'	11 Esc	Crashed near Trembecourt, France.

15/03/91	E17 '7-PN'	7 Esc	Crashed 10 miles from St Dizier following a bird strike.
28/05/91	A142	Esc	Crashed.
29/08/91	XX843 'GT'	54 Sqn	Crashed following a mid-air collision with a Cessna 152 over Carno, near Newtown, Powys, Wales.
27/10/91	205	8 Sqn	Crashed 5 miles south of Masirah.
17/12/91	207	8 Sqn	Crashed west of the Jebel range following a bird strike.
13/06/92	A65 '7-IS'	7 Esc	Crashed on take-off from Ndjamena, Chad, after ingesting a bird.
15/09/92	A95 '11-MQ'	11 Esc	Crashed near Mont de Marsan.
22/08/93	A83 '11-MT'	11 Esc	Crashed north-east of Biltine, Chad.
16/09/93	E38 '7-PM'	7 Esc	Crashed near Bar-le-Duc, Meuse, France.
24/02/94	A12 '7-IF'	7 Esc	Crashed in Captieux range, Landes area of south-west France.
01/08/94	A119	11 Esc	Crashed in Central African Republic.
14/09/94	E27 '11-'	11 Esc	Crashed near Diane-Capelle, France.
12/01/95	A31 '7-PW'	7 Esc	Crashed near Vitroy-le-Francois, France.
22/03/95	E16 '11-MS'	11 Esc	Crashed near Chalon-sur-Saone while participating in Exercise Datex 95.
22/03/95		IAF	Crashed on take-off from Ambala Air Base, India.
21/06/95	XZ373 'GF'	54 Sqn	Crashed over the Adriatic during an ACM sortie.
25/06/95	JS 161	IAF	Crashed.
17/10/95		IAF	Crashed close to the India/Pakistan border at Rajasthan.
23/01/96	XX733 'ER'	6 Sqn	Crashed on take-off from Coltishall.
03/06/96	A44 '11-MC'	11 Esc	Crashed near Bar-le-Duc, France.
24/07/96	XZ362 'GC'	54 Sqn	Crashed in Alaska while being flown by a 41 Sqn pilot during Exercise Cope Thunder.
12/08/96	JS 167	IAF	Crashed on take-off from Ambala Air Base.
18/09/96	XX143 'X'	16 (R) Sqn	Crashed into Moray Firth shortly after take-off from Lossiemouth.
03/09/98	XZ108 'GL'	54 Sqn	Crashed 12 miles off Norfolk coast during an ACM sortie.
24/02/99	A97 '7-HR'	7 Esc	Crashed 25km from Bar-le-Duc during an ACM sortie.
30/06/99		IAF	Crashed in the Punjab, India.
20/09/99		IAF	Crashed into buildings in Utter Pradesh state.
20/10/99	XZ381 'EC'	16 (R) Sqn	Crashed 6 miles north of Lossiemouth into the Moray Firth, following hydraulic failure.
08/11/99		16 or 27 Sqn IAF	Crashed in Gorakhpur district, Utter Pradesh state, India.
27/10/00	XZ111 'GO'	54 Sqn	Crashed 5 miles north-east Dumfries following a bird strike.
25/07/01	XZ363 'FO'	41 Sqn	Crashed in Alaska while being flown by a 54 Sqn pilot during Exercise Cope Thunder.
19/11/01	E39	Esc	Crashed.
09/05/02		IAF	Crashed at Ambala Air Base, India.
29/01/03		IAF	Crashed over Mahrajan firing range in Bikaner district, India.

Jaguar T.2 XX832 'U' of 226 OCU seen at RAF Lossiemouth on 20 August 1975. Whilst operating with No.6 Squadron from Hahn air base in Germany, the jet struck high tension wires on 7 August 1988 with the loss of the pilot. The USAF officer in the rear cockpit ejected safely.

22/07/03		IAF	Crashed on take-off from Ambala Air Base following an in-flight fire.
26/02/04		IAF	Crashed near Chandhan range, India.
02/04/04		IAF	Crashed in Himalayas, northern Kashmir.
02/04/04		IAF	Crashed in Himalayas, northern Kashmir.

07/05/04		IAF	Crashed near Ambala Air Base, India.
11/05/05		IAF	Crashed 30km north-west of Gorakhour Air Base, Utter Pradesh, India.
07/10/05		IAF	Crashed on outskirts of Gwalior Air Base, India.

During Exercise Cope Thunder on 25 July 2001, XZ363, a Jaguar GR.3, being operated by No.54 (F) Squadron but belonging to No.41 (F) Squadron, crashed. It is seen here in its desert pink colour scheme for Operation Warden during September 1991.

Escadra Jaguar E E17/7-PN seen landing at Orange on 28 May 1989. This aircraft was lost near St Dizier following a bird strike on 15 March 1991.

Jaguar GR.1 XZ362 '27' of No.II (AC) Squadron, seen on the right in this picture, was lost in Alaska during a Cope Thunder exercise on 24 July 1996 while on strength of No.54 (F) Squadron. The pilot, from No.41 (F) Squadron, ejected safely.

CHAPTER 8

WHEN IT REALLY IS NOT YOUR DAY

SITTING IN A car driving from RAF St Mawgan to a hotel in Newquay in September 1989 I was chatting with John Whitehead and Rick Lea, the two pilots I had flown down with from RNAS Yeovilton earlier in the day. I am not sure how the subject got around to plastic surgery, but a throwaway comment from John Whitehead – 'You cannot even see the join' – when referring to Rick Lea prompted me to ask what he was on about. It was from this that the story unfolded.

Rick Lea was a very experienced fast-jet pilot, earning his living by flying with the Fleet Requirement Air Direction Unit (FRADU) as a contract pilot. Formerly RAF and more latterly the RAAF where he flew Mirage III EOs Rick had returned to 'civilian' life when it was made clear that the 'Pom' was not going on to F/A-18A Hornets. At that time he joined 'Airwork' I believe as an instructor pilot on Hunter aircraft with the then Sultan of Oman Air Force (SOAF).

On arriving in Oman, his new 'boss' was Air Commodore Eric Bennett and Rick found himself transferred to the Jaguar programme. One day in February 1979 Rick was tasked with putting the Jaguar through its paces at a firepower demonstration held not too far from the Jaguar's main operating base at Thumrait.

Flying in aircraft 212 a number of ordnance deliveries were carried out demonstrating weapon-aiming using laser ranging. On the final run Rick was to deliver a 500lb Pakistani-made bomb with pinpoint accuracy on to the target. The weapon, I would add, had not been trialled or approved by BAE SYSTEMS and had been absorbed into the Jaguar's arsenal locally. The aircraft commenced its attack and the bomb was 'pickled' at the appropriate moment but, as it cleared the aircraft, it detonated prematurely having somehow fused in flight.

The force of the explosion within such close proximity to the aircraft ruptured all main systems and caused the aircraft to break up in mid-air into three distinct segments. The ensuing explosion ruptured the aircrafts 'LOX' container (liquid oxygen) immediately to the left-hand underside of the ejection seat. This in turn caused a fireball in the cockpit through which Rick Lea ejected.

Sitting in that car in Cornwall, Rick recounted the story as though it were an everyday occurrence. He went on to say that, as his parachute opened, he felt his arms, leg and face all stinging from the burns that he received. His next realisation was that he could not see, but this turned out to be burnt skin covering his eyes.

Although at a range area a good distance from any hospital, a number of helicopters were available, due to the demonstration having been for high-ranking officials. Rick was quickly rescued

Rick Lea, who was involved in the almost tragic loss of Omani 'OS10', is seen here in September 1989, having recovered from his injuries, at the controls of a FRADU Hunter GA.11 (XE685) taxiing to his parking spot at RAF St Mawgan.

Royal Air Force of Oman Jaguar Internationals seen over the Jebel. Leading is 'OB3' No.214, one of the two RAFO twin-seat Jaguars to be fitted for in-flight refuelling.

and carried into a helicopter and then flown to Masirah. Air Commodore Bennett accompanied him and Rick said he could see the aircraft's loadmaster trying to make him comfortable, but there were tears rolling down his face.

He said: 'I knew it must be my condition that was having that effect. I also must in my own mind have known how badly injured I was because I turned to Air Commodore Bennett and said: "Eric [and you don't use the boss' first name lightly], don't ever ask me to do that again, it was f*****g dangerous!!!"'

Rick Lea was lucky to survive such an accident and he did so firstly because of his good physical condition (a lesser person would probably have died from his injuries), and, secondly, through his training and reflexes. The post-accident investigation discovered, amongst other things, that the fireball in the cockpit had burnt through the drogue gun connection to the parachute. They calculated in such a temperature it would have taken just three seconds to sever it completely. Rick Lea ejected two seconds after the bomb exploded.

The last I heard of Rick was that he was flying hot air balloons in the West Country.

CHAPTER 9

JAGUAR MAINTENANCE SERIALS

8563M	XW563	Displayed RAF Coltishall as 'XX822'.
8600M	XX761	Preserved Boscombe Down (cockpit only).
8815M	XX118	L/N Abingdon dump 02/92.
8816M	XX734	Preserved Gatwick Aviation Museum, Charlwood.
8821M	XX115	No.1 SoTT RAF Cosford.
8895M	XX746	No.1 SoTT RAF Cosford.
8896M	XX821	Aircraft Maintenance Instruction Flight, RAF Cranwell.
8897M	XX969	No.1 SoTT RAF Cosford.
8898M	XX119	Allocated but not taken up.
8899M	XX756	No.1 SoTT RAF Cosford.
8900M	XZ368	No.1 SoTT RAF Cosford.
8901M	XZ383	No.1 SoTT RAF Cosford.
8902M	XX739	No.1 SoTT RAF Cosford.
8903M	XX747	Aircraft Maintenance Instruction Flight, RAF Cranwell.
8904M	XX966	No.1 SoTT RAF Cosford.
8905M	XX975	No.1 SoTT RAF Cosford.
8906M	XX976	No.1 SoTT RAF Cosford.
8907M	XZ371	No.1 SoTT RAF Cosford.
8908M	XZ382	Preserved Bruntingthorpe, Leicestershire.
8918M	XX109	Preserved City of Norwich Museum.
8923M	XX819	No.1 SoTT RAF Cosford.
8937M	XX751	No.1 SoTT RAF Cosford.
8945M	XX818	No.1 SoTT RAF Cosford.
8946M	XZ389	No.1 SoTT RAF Cosford.
8947M	XX726	No.1 SoTT RAF Cosford.
8948M	XX757	No.1 SoTT RAF Cosford.
8949M	XX743	No.1 SoTT RAF Cosford.
8950M	XX956	No.1 SoTT RAF Cosford.
8951M	XX727	No.1 SoTT RAF Cosford.
8952M	XX730	No.1 SoTT RAF Cosford.
8953M	XX959	No.1 SoTT RAF Cosford.
8954M	XZ384	No.1 SoTT RAF Cosford.
8955M	XX110	No.1 SoTT RAF Cosford.
8978M	XX837	No.1 SoTT RAF Cosford.
9003M	XZ390	No.1 SoTT RAF Cosford.
9004M	XZ370	No.1 SoTT RAF Cosford.
9005M	XZ374	No.1 SoTT RAF Cosford.
9006M	XX967	No.1 SoTT RAF Cosford.

9007M	XX968	No.1 SoTT RAF Cosford.
9008M	XX140	L/N Park Aviation & Supply 03/05.
9009M	XX763	DARA Apprentice Training School, RAF St Athan.
9010M	XX764	DARA Apprentice Training School, RAF St Athan.
9019M	XX824	No.1 SoTT RAF Cosford.
9020M	XX825	No.1 SoTT RAF Cosford.
9021M	XX826	No.1 SoTT RAF Cosford, but up for disposal.
9022M	XX958	No.1 SoTT RAF Cosford.
9023M	XX844	L/N dumped at St Athan 09/99.
9087M	XX753	RAF Exhibition Flight (cockpit only).
9110M	XX736	BAE SYSTEMS Brough (nose and tail section only).
9132M	XX977	Aircraft Recovery & Transportation Flight, St Athan.
9251M	XX746?	No.1 SoTT RAF Cosford.
9252M	XX721?	
9254M	XX965	Aircraft Maintenance Instruction Flight, RAF Cranwell.
9255M	XZ375	Preserved Coltishall (nose section only).
9256M	XX839	L/N Conifer Metals, Clay Cross, Chesterfield 05/02.
9257M	XX962	No.1 SoTT RAF Cosford.
9262M	XZ358	Aircraft Maintenance Instruction Flight, RAF Cranwell.
9266M	XZ119	Aircraft Maintenance Instruction Flight, RAF Cranwell.
9282M	XZ101	Ground Instructional Airframe, QinetiQ Boscombe Down.
9293M	XX830	Preserved at Coltishall (cockpit only).
9297M	XX141	Aircraft Maintenance Instruction Flight, RAF Cranwell.
9306M	XX979	Aircraft Maintenance Instruction Flight, RAF Cranwell.

The Aircraft Maintenance Instruction Flight introduces ab initio technicians to first line servicing and aircraft dispatch. In this shot can be seen Jaguar XX141, GRIA X2119 and GRI XX821

CHAPTER 10

THE FRENCH CONNECTION – Armee De l'Air

ALTHOUGH THIS BOOK concerns itself with UK-built aircraft because it is of an Anglo–French design, passing reference to its use within the Armee de l'Air has to be made.

The original agreement between France and Great Britain on production of Jaguar saw a requirement for each company to build 200 examples. Whereas in the United Kingdom great efforts were made to secure an export market in France following the takeover of Breguet by Dassault, little or nothing was done to promote the aircraft. True to form, Dassault effectively killed the joint project so as not to compete against its own often inferior products.

That said, the Armee de l'Air, akin to the Royal Air Force, came to appreciate the rugged and reliable Jaguar, with the type bearing the brunt of much of the overseas out-of-theatre operations, particularly in the French African colonies. The aircraft did not enjoy the degree of upgrades that RAF aircraft received but were, from the outset, designed to deploy a wider range of munitions. In spite of remaining in service until 2005, they remained very much the poor relation in the Jaguar world.

Two complete fighter-bomber wings, 7 and 11 Escadre de Chasse, and one squadron, Escuadron de Chasse 3/3, were to equip with the Jaguar, together with a number of miscellaneous units.

Escuadron de Chasse 3/3 'Ardennes' at Base Aeriennes 133 Nancy-Ochey re-equipped with the Jaguar between March and October 1977 but saw only limited service with the aircraft, transitioning to the Mirage IIIE in June 1987. Its role was attack and its primary munition was the BAe/MATRA AS37 Martel anti-radar missile.

The component squadrons of 7 Escadre de Chasse, Escuadron de Chasse 1/7 'Provence', along with EC 3/7 'Languedoc' at Base Aerienne 113 St Dizier/Robinson and EC 4/7 'Limousin' at Base Aerienne 125 Istres/Le Tube, were assigned to tactical nuclear strike with the French AN52 weapon. EC2/7 'Argonne', also at St Dizier, undertook the task of type and operational conversion.

The squadrons were declared operational on the Jaguar on 1 September 1974, 1 July 1975, 1 April 1980 and 11 October 1974 respectively although the AN52 was down declared from service on 1 September 1991, at which point the Jaguars reverted to their previous secondary task of conventional attack.

EC01.007, as it became, was the final French user of the Jaguar, flying the final examples into storage at Chateaudun on 1 July 2005. The wing is scheduled to become the first AdlA unit to re-equip with Rafale.

EC02.007 and EC03.007 both inactivated on Jaguar on 8 June 2001, while the detached EC4/7 transitioned to the Dassault Mirage 2000N within 4 Wing on 31 July 1989.

Escuadron de Chasse 1/11 'Roussillon' was declared operational on the Jaguar at Toul-Rossieres on 1 March 1976, its role conventional in support of the French 1st Army. EC2/11 'Vosges'

7 Escadra Jaguar A A5/7-PK seen at Cambrai on 5 June 1978.

11 Escadra Jaguar A A160/11-RT sporting a desert colour scheme, seen on 11 March 1992. This was the last French Jaguar built.

11 Escadra Jaguar A A89/11-RE seen on approach on 4 October 1994.

7 Escadra Jaguar A A14/7-PG seen at Orange on 28 May 1989.

stood up on Jaguar on 1 June 1977 and was tasked with suppression of enemy air defences (SEAD). EC3/11 'Corse', who formed on 7 February 1975, and the detached EC4/11 'Jura' at Bordeaux, from 1 August 1978, were attached to Force d'Action Exterieure for overseas out-of-theatre operations. It was these two units, until 30 June1992 when the latter disbanded, that bore the brunt of French Colonial support.

Apart from the test and experimental units of CEV and CEAM, the final French user of the Jaguar was the Centre d'Instruction Tactique 339 at Luxeuil/St Sauveur. Here, five twin-seat Jaguar Es, along with a couple of CM.170 Fouga Magisters and radar equipped Mystere 20s, undertook tactical navigation training. The Jaguars provided the fast jet low-level input.

11 Escadra Jaguar A A148/11-YL in desert scheme at RAF Waddington on 2 May 1985.

ZB615 was the last Jaguar built for the home market, undertaking its first flight on 23 September 1982 – almost a decade after XX108. This was procured for the RAE and ETPS and was retired just over two years after XX108. The advent of digital photography has created unlimited opportunities. This shot was taken using a Nikon D.100 with a 300mm focal length Nikkor 4.5 lens at 650th of a second on RAW.

If you are interested in purchasing other books published by Tempus,
or in case you have difficulty finding any Tempus books in your local bookshop,
you can also place orders directly through our website

www.tempus-publishing.com